Bassana-Richard FOROT

RIGHTS AND DUTIES OF TENANTS AND LANDLORDS IN FRANCE

lulu Edition
www.lulu.com

From the same author (French publications):

Propreté et gestion des déchets à Paris hier et aujourd'hui. France, Editions Bénévent, mars 2007, 90 p.

Location de logement dans le secteur privé et recueil de jurisprudence, Ed. lulu 2ᵉ trimestre 2007, 140 p.

Lulu Edition, 2nd quarter 2009
www.lulu.com

ISBN: **978-1-4092-9143-5**

CONTENTS

INTRODUCTION

The law of 6 July 1989, its revisions and ordinances essentially govern renting accommodation in the private sector. The installation of tenant in the premises shall be formalized by the signing Contract, which will be the focus of this book. Owners and tenants conclude renew leases with or without the aid of a specialist. In both cases it is necessary to have knowledge of much of the law, operation of contracts that bind to each other and prevent conflicts when the parties recourse to the conciliation commission or a passage before the judge. Even if transaction amicably, the prior knowledge of some decisions of judges on the subject informs and facilitates negotiation. As specialists in real estate, representatives of owners or tenants - unions or associations - lawyers and various experts, they can very quickly find in this book first information, and have the possibility eventually rising to the law itself and complete original texts proposed and whose elements are each time referenced in the book. The lease is discussed in three aspects:
- The bulk of the Act of July 6 on main objects.
- Examples of case law on these objects
-The procedures and steps to fixed rent renew a lease successful conciliation or, last resort to the court.
 Concerning in particular the European Court, Decisions of judges are organized as follows:
First, examples of cases are classified the most recent to the oldest and thus allow not only to monitor the decision on some objects, but also to identify some contradictions to the level of the Court of Cassation. In addition, each time when the case is this, the court's ruling is the latest privileged.
Then I wanted to diversify the decisions in court, which covers a wider range material and tends to show that judicial decision is not always with the same sensitivity or interpretation everywhere.

French law, decisions in litigation can be rented for three levels of courts will be reflected throughout the book, so here, as a preamble, a summary of the hierarchical jurisdiction of such courts.

Jurisdiction and hierarchy of courts in matters of French rental lease:

Magistrates Court

General competence for small civil disputes

The Magistrates Court deals with most of the small civil disputes of everyday life. The court considers all civil matters for which application is made for amounts less than or equal to 10 000: litigation-related traffic accidents, disputes concerning the payment of condominium fees, unpaid debts, supply non-compliant, poorly executed work , claims for damages or reimbursement of a product or service....

Exclusive jurisdiction in certain cases it shall act on a series of cases, whatever the amount requested. For example:

• disputes between landlords and tenants on housing: payment of rent, termination of lease... actions called "possessory" to enforce the possession or possession of a property such as respect of an easement of way;

• attacks on funerals or for tuition or internship;

• disputes relating to pruning trees and hedges and actions to fix the boundary limits of two properties;

 • attacks on political elections (compilation of voter lists) and elections within companies...

It also disputes relating to consumer credit in an amount less than or equal to 21 346.86 Euros (ex: credit for the purchase of a car or a kitchen ...).

Court of Appeal

Competence: a review of cases already tried once the appellate court reviews the cases already tried in the first degree (1st or spring 1st instance) in civil, commercial, social or criminal.

 It reviews the decisions:

• of the court (for cases where the amount of the demand for justice is more than 4 000 where the sum is determined);
• the High Court;
• the Commercial Court;
• the industrial tribunal (cases with a value greater than 4 000 Euros);
• Court of joint tenancies;
• Court Social Security;
• the police court regarding violations of 5th grade;
• the criminal court;
• the judge (the court of appeal then meets in a chamber of instruction).

Exception: Appeals from decisions of assize courts were tried by another court of assize (law of 15 June 2000 strengthening the presumption of innocence and the rights of victims, supplemented by an Act of 4 March 2002).

The appellate court exercises control by law and in fact on the judgments that are submitted. It can confirm the decision of the Court of First Instance or the reverse (i.e. cancel, the reform) in completely or in part. In the latter case, the new installment to the substance.

The judgments rendered by the appellate courts may be subject to an appeal brought before the Supreme Court.

The Supreme Court

The Supreme Court is the highest court of the judiciary in France. The Supreme Court, established by the Constituent Assembly in 1790 during the French Revolution, preceded it. Sitting in the Courthouse in Paris, the Supreme Court's mission to review, at the request of the parties, the decisions by courts and courts of appeals in both criminal and civil (including 3 civil) . The Court leaves open the questions of law or law enforcement; it did not consider the facts. It provides its jurisprudence on harmonious laws. Since 1991, the Court, at the request of the courts, gives its opinion on questions of law and complex new arising in many cases.

CHAPTER I

GIVEN LEAVE BY THE OWNER OR LESSEE

Most of the law

Leave to live or to sell the dwelling or a legitimate and serious is one of the major events of the lease. We note that the notification of the leave, including the tenant, until his final performance very difficult, if we judge by the number of appeals to courts and the interventions of the Supreme Court, as well leave is a legal document that must be particular care in form and substance in based on the occasion, the existing jurisprudence.

The notification requirements and procedures of the leave are in Article 15 of Chapter II of the Act of July 6 1989, reproduced below, with changes by the following laws.

Article 15-I: When the owner gives leave to his tenant, such leave must be justified by its decision to resume or sell housing, or by a ground legitimate and serious, including failure by the tenant of one of its obligations. A penalty of nullity, the given leave by the owner must state the grounds claimed and, in case of recovery, the name and address of the recipient recovery that cannot be the donor, his spouse, "the partner to whom he is bound by a civil solidarity pact recorded on the date of discharge "(Act n ° 99-944 of 15 November 1999, Article 14-III), known for his partner at least one year from the date of leave, his parents, his descendants or those of his spouse, his partner "(Act n ° 99-944 of 15 November 1999, Article 14 -IV) or its well-known partner. The notice period applicable to the leave is three months when made by the tenant and six months when it emanates from the lessor. However, in case of mutation or loss of employment "Or new

11

employment resulting from a loss of employment (Law No. 94-624 of 21 July 1994 Article 14-III), the tenant may give the owner with a notice period be reduced to a month.

The time is also reduced to one month for tenants aged over sixty years whose health warrants a change of domicile "as well as the beneficiaries of minimum income "(Act No. 90-449 31 May 1990).

Leave must be notified by letter with return receipt requested or served by a bailiff act. This period from the date of receipt of the letter recommended or the notification of the bailiff. During the period of notice, the tenant is liable for rent and expenses for the time he actually places where the lessor has notified the leave. It is liable to pay the rent and expenses on all period of notice if he has notified the leave, unless the housing is occupied by the end of the notice by a tenant in accordance with the donor.

At the expiry of the notice period, the tenant is deprived of any evidence of occupation of rented premises. Article 15-II. When it is based on the decision to sell the housing, the leave must, on pain of nullity, and the price conditions of the proposed sale. The leave is offering sale to the tenant: The offer is valid during the first two months of the notice period. "The provisions of Article 4 of Law No 65-557 of 10 July 1965 laying down the status of the condominium buildings are not applicable leave based on the decision to sell the housing "(Act n ° 2000-1208 of 13 December 2000, Article 190-I). At the expiry of the notice, the tenant who has not accepted the offer of sale shall be deprived of any right under occupation on the premises.

A tenant who has accepted the offer, from the date sending its response to the lessor within two months for the completion of the sale. If, in its response, it notifies its intention to use a loan, the acceptance by the tenant of the sale offer is conditional on obtaining the loan and the deadline for completion of the sale was extended to four months. The lease is extended until deadline for completion of the sale. If at the expiry of that period, the sale was not made, acceptance of the offer sale is void and the tenant is deprived of any right as an occupation. "If the owner decides to sell to conditions or at a lower price for the acquirer, the notary must notify the tenant of these conditions and prices barely invalidity of the sale. »The tenant to the owner makes this notification to the address for this purpose if the tenant did not know this address to the lessor; the notification is made at the premises where lease had been granted. It is offer for sale to tenant. This offer is valid for a period of one month from its receipt. The offer was not accepted in one-month fell.

The tenant accepts the offer and has notified to from the sending of its response to the lessor or the notary, a period of two months for carrying out the act of sale. If in its response it shall notify its intention to use for a loan, a tenant by the acceptance of the offer of sale is subject to obtaining the loan and the implementation period

the sale was extended to four months. If at the expiration of this time the sale was not made, acceptance of the offer sale is invalid. The terms of the five preceding paragraphs are reproduced in void in each notification (Act No. 94-64 of 1 July 1994, Article 15-I). These provisions do not apply to acts occurring between relatives up to third degree inclusive, under the condition that the purchaser occupies the accommodation for a period not less than two years, from the expiry of the notice, or to acts on the buildings mentioned in the second paragraph of Article 1 of Law No. 53-286 of 4 April 1953 amending Law No. 48-1360 of 1 September 1948, amending and codification of legislation on reporting from owners and tenants or occupants of residential premises or for professional   use.

"In the case of leave provided for sale 11-1, supply sale to the tenant is dissociated leave (Law No. 2000-1208 of 13 December 2000).

Article 15-III. The owner can not oppose the renewal of the contract by giving the leave conditions specified in paragraph 1 above in respect of any tenant who is over seventy years and whose Annual income is less than one and a half times the annual minimum wage increase, without a home for its needs and possibilities to be offered within the geographic boundaries Article 13 bis of Law No. 48-1360 of 1 September 1948 above

However, the provisions of the preceding paragraph are not apply where the lessor is an individual aged over sixty years and its annual are less than one and a half times the annual minimum wage growth. The age of the tenant and the owner are valued at Contract expiry date, the amount of their resources is assessed at the date of notification of the leave.

Examples of case law

2001. Tenant notice of unemployment: in principle three months, the period of notice the tenant shall be reduced to one month in case of job loss resulting from a period unemployment, among others. The Supreme Court refused to equate the lack of jobs to job loss. She estimated that an unemployed person is not entitled to notice Short: "the mere absence of employment is not part of If the situation referred to Article 15-I, paragraph 2 of the Act of 6 July 1989 for the benefit of one month's notice. » Supreme Court, 3 rd Civil Chamber, 4 April 2001.

2001.The right of recovery involves the lessor to use housing as his residence Primary: the Supreme Court states for this owner who had wanted to return to his home use it as a pied-à-terre "that the right to resume required the lessor of the premises housing the principal purpose and not second homes. » Supreme Court, 3rd Civil Chamber, 31 January 2001.

2001. Shape of the letter of notice of the tenant: breaking an appeal decision, the Supreme Court requires tenant to give leave in the same manner that the Lessor: letter charged with receiving. Supreme Court, 3rd Civil Chamber, decision of 3 April 2001.

2001. Leave described as "fraudulent": having found that the lessor, who had to leave recovery, under Article 15-I of the Act of July 6 1989, and who, less than seven months after the takeover, a given to lease housing to others for rent substantially higher, not justify the setting location by the loss of employment of his son or his wife, an appellate court was entitled, in its appeal Sovereign of assessment, evidence of the fraudulent of recovery:

- "Considering, first, that the Court of Appeal sovereignty decided that the apartment had been given to leased to third in June 1996, less than 7 months after the takeover, for a rent of 765 Euros monthly, or 270% of rent paid by the tenant, the owner will justify the introduction of location in a loss employment of his son or his wife and that the speed of relocation sufficiently demonstrated the fraudulent of the recovery.

- And, secondly, that the Court of Appeal supremely appreciated the amount of damage it justified by the existence in the evaluation made, where it follows that the plea is unfounded, for these reasons, rejects the appeal. "Supreme Court, 3rd Civil Chamber, Case 3 April 2001.

2001. Leave notified before the reality of the division lots is illegal and void: leave granted to sell by the lessor prior to the division of the lots is void for lack of purpose, without any necessary to take into account the failure of the annexation leave the settlement of ownership or the description of places. "At the date of discharge there was no settlement established ownership of the draft Regulation of condominiums and description of division coming just been established. » Court of Appeal de Paris, 6 the Chamber B, 26 April 2001.

2001. Leave illegal and verification: having found that the owner had granted a leave tenant for living accommodation, under the law 6 July 1989, Article 15-I, no justification or occupation personal site for a period of five months after notified to leave, or any event unable to justify the occupation, an appellate court has lawfully, without reversing the burden of proof, remember the responsibility of the owner and ordered to compensate his former tenant. Supreme Court, 3rd Civil Chamber, 21 February 2001.

2000. The method of calculating the income of the tenant more than 70 years on income assessed separately each tenant, which means that if one of them is below the legal threshold, the protection is gained. After a few opinions in the past, Court rules for the separate assessment of income the couple married. Supreme Court, 3rd Civil Chamber, Case 19 July 2000.

2000. Leave for sale and scope of the overestimation of the price: the price is excessive not sufficient by itself to prove the fraud. "Having noted that the selling price of the apartment of a dependent building built 34 years ago, in an area enjoying all the amenities, corresponding to 112 % of the estimate of the expert, the Court of Appeal sovereignty decided that this award was not excessive or deterrent and that the fraudulent intent of the owner could not result of his desire to make a modest profit selling his property. » Supreme Court, 3rd Civil Chamber, Case 19 April 2000.

2000. The evidence of the leave: owner had served on the tenant leave based on his intention to sell her home. The leave was canceled for the following reasons: the owner had intended prevent fraudulent occupier to exercise its pre-emption right, the price being offered voluntarily deterrent; also the owner never gave

Sales to a real estate agent and finally had not shown that potential buyers had visited the site or a proposal to purchase. The lease was

extended to the tenant. Supreme Court, 3rd Civil Chamber, 15 March 2000.

2000. The accuracy of the relationship of the recipient is not required during the leave The Act of July 6 allows the owner to give the tenant to take shelter for himself, his spouse, ascendants or descendants, the leave must then indicate the name and address of the recipient recovery but it is not required to specify the link kinship between the donor and the recipient. Court of Cassation, 3rd Civil Chamber, 2 February 2000.

2000. The invalidity of leave for non-precision local annexes: An owner has notified a tenant leave by failing to mention the presence a cave with rented housing. The Court of Appeal Due to the tenant and accordingly cancels leave grounds that the offer of sale was neither accurate nor devoid ambiguity as to its purpose. The court confirmed the arrest and rejects the claims of the owner. The Court also had the opportunity to cancel leave because it omitted to mention the garage. Supreme Court, 3rd Civil Chamber, 21 June 2000.

2000. Damages, the remaining housing vacant after a leave to dwell: the owner a home had to leave but resumed four months after the departure of the tenant, housing was still vacant. The former tenant was awarded damages and leave interest fraudulent. The Supreme Court that "the owner had never been apartment on the departure of the tenant, invoking reasons which do not characterize the existence of a cause self-justifying that failure. » Supreme Court, 3rd Civil Chamber, 19 April 2000.

2000. Damages for wrongful leave an owner has granted leave to sell, the tenant has unable to use its right of first refusal and had to leave places. Shortly after leaving the owner rented housing arguing that the sale did not take place Due to extensive repairs. The judge accepted the bad faith, the owner in finding that the price of sale was excessive in comparison to market values and that housing was mainly rented without delay, with a amount of only 1 220 Euros. The former tenant has thereby obtained 3 810 Euros in damages and interests. Court of Appeal of Montpellier, 11 January 2000.

2000. Leave for home, period of occupation places at the discretion of judges: the daughter of an owner had moved only after the execution of renovations, which had begun 16 months after the release of housing by tenants. Considering that the recovery had not been made within reasonable, the appeals judges agreed with the judge's instance to have ordered the owner to pay his former tenants compensation of 7135 Euros for material, characterized by three years of extra Monthly rent of 200 Euros and up to 760 Euros, under the pain and suffering. They refused to condemn the former tenants the cost of repairs damaged the lock when the witness authorized to request them. Paris Court of Appeal, 6

Case 5 the September 2000.

2000. Leave a tenant under lease and solidarity clause: owners who rent to unmarried persons should not forget that the clause solidarity stipulated in the contract has its limits. The Chamber who gave his leave shall be held by this solidarity clause, the obligation to pay rent in full until the expiry of the lease on the date of the leave. If the lease is automatically renewed with co-owner tenant remained, only the latter remain required to pay the rents and charges: one of notified its tenants leave on 18 April 1994, when that the lease expired on 2 June 1995. The Supreme Court considered after this ate, the solidarity could not be invoked against the former tenant. Court of Cassation, 3rd Civil Chamber, decision of 12 July 2000.

2000. Case of rejection of the serious and legitimate reason invoked by the owner: a common stated wish to recover a dwelling to achieve housing for youth in the region. However, it had proved,

to the evidence on record that the real intention of the town was to sell the land to a company credit. Leave a sale would have allowed the tenant to use its right of first refusal and to purchase, which would have prevented the town to realize its project. The court felt "that the town had relied on an alleged serious and legitimate reason to hide his intent to sell, by extension, the land containing the

rented accommodation and had engaged in a misuse of Article 15-I of the Act of 6 July 1989. Supreme Court, 3rd Civil Chamber, 19 January 2000.

2000. No compensation is capital due to leave at the sale: a company insurance required by the recording without delay of 10% the selling price of housing in the wake of a leave sale and the tenant, using its right of preemption, had decided to acquire the

Supreme Court quashed the leave and extended the lease for 6 years and has estimated "By imposing obligations on spouses tenants, if acceptance of the offer of sale, record as allowance of 10% of asset sales price, insurance company had to leave on 20 June 1995 Short on time to the tenant to collect the funds. " Supreme Court, 3rd Civil Chamber, 1 March 2000.

2000. Termination of tenancy and housing rights: the right to housing cannot create any obligation by reposing the lessor has obtained the termination of the lease at the fault of tenant for non-compliance with its obligations. Court of Appeal de Paris, 6 the Chamber B, 23 March 2000. 1999. Reduced notice to leave because Health: tenants aged over sixty years, including state of health justifies a change of address may rely on the reduced period of notice. Court of Appeal Toulouse, 3rd Chamber, 19 January 1999.

1999. Leave for sale, should indicate the housing area (Law of 18 December Carrez 1996)? The courts have asked the question and after some hesitation, existing case law does not the owner that states this area. Supreme Court, 3rd Civil Chamber, decision of 3 July 1999.

1999. Leave for sale in the entire building: when the owner sells the property in its entirety, it does may grant leave to sell the space currently occupied by the tenant. The Supreme Court ruled on   the nullity of holiday sales, indicating the price and conditions Sales for the entire property. Supreme Court, 3rd Civil Chamber, 13 July   1999.

1998. Notice of leave and dismissal negotiated: even if his dismissal was negotiated, the tenant benefits from reduced notice referred to in Article 15 paragraph 2-I the Law of 6 July 1989. Court of Appeal of Paris, 6 the Chamber 10 February 1998.

1998. The mutation of the companion does not right to notice reduced to one month: the mutation a professional partner cannot allow the other member of the couple to receive a notice reduced. Court of Appeal of Aix-en-Provence, 11 e Chamber, 26 February 1998.

1998. Extension of the concept of descendant: the adopted simply must be seen as a descendant and can therefore, as such, enjoy the right of recovery referred to in Article 19 of the 1948 Act - the law should be extended the law of 6 July 1989 -. Supreme Court, 3rd Chamber civil, 22 April 1998.

1998. A reasonable time after the occupation leave taken: Although the Act of July 6 does not the period, within which the recovery should take place it must within a reasonable time. Court, Paris, 7 January 1998.

1998. Flexibility of assessment of the period of recovery: the court held that a three-month occupation by the beneficiary of the recovery, preceded by ten-month fraud. Supreme Court, 3rd Civil Chamber, 18 November 1998.

1998. Period of notice for employment of a tenant in fixed-term contract: if loss of employment, the tenant who leaves his home is right to give one month's notice to the owner instead of three months allowed by law. The tenant without employment after a fixed term contract can - he qualifies for reduced notice? In such a case, the Supreme Court refused to reduce to one-month duration of notice, because the tenant knew, at days of signing the lease, his contract length determined would certainly take a few days late later. Supreme Court, 3rd Civil Case 30 September 1998.

1998. Contestation of the tenant leave by the tenant is locked in a period of two months for accept or refuse the offer of selling leave sale. The action contesting leave the tenant was subject to any period, the tenant may rely on the irregularities affecting the leave, despite the effect of it. Supreme Court, 3rd Civil Chamber, 7 October 1998.

1998. The income of the tenant of more than 70 years do suffer no reduction in the Supreme Court confirms that in the event of leave, the resources to take consideration (annual value of less than one and half the annual minimum wage) are those reported to before the tax abatement or deduction not net income. Above all, she said that when the tenant is married, no deduction is to be applied in Because of the family situation of the lessee; the fact that only husband had income did not practice abatement of 50% as the couple argued tenant. Supreme Court, 3rd Civil Chamber, decision of 18 February 1998.

1998. Leave given by a representative of the owner: leave given by an agent must mention the name (or name) of the lessor. The words "in the name and on behalf of the owner which does not specify the identity of the lessor fails to meet this obligation and entails the revocation of leave granted for sale under such conditions. Supreme Court, Assembly plenary, 13 February 1998.

1998. Leave and tenant relocation of the Court Appeal violated Article III-15 holding that the failure to offer of local replacement does not leave the void, but the renders unenforceable only to the lessee as a housing it is not proposed when the contract ended before the proposed new Housing has been renewed. Supreme Court, 3rd Chamber Civil, 1st July 1998.

1998. Solidarity in the payment of rent: solidarity in the lease does not oblige the lessor to claim the unpaid rent to two tenants, on the contrary, it allows him to contact debtors that he wants to choose, without it could raise against the benefits of division and is in tenant to turn to his co to claim possibly a contribution. Supreme Court, 3rd Civil

Chamber 24 June 1998.

1997. The case of a transfer from one district to the other, Paris intra walls: court held that the transfer to another district of the same city does not imply a change of residence justifying reducing the period of notice. Paris, 6 the Chamber, March 27 1997.

1997. Reprise unauthorized nephews to: the Paris Court of Appeal said that the terms of Article 15 the Law of 6 July 1989, the nephews were not among beneficiaries of the upturn to live and that the article cannot be interpreted strictly, as a provision of public order. Court of Appeal of Paris, 6 the Chamber B, 11March 1997.

1997. The income to be taken into account are regular: the Court stated that "should be taken into the regular resources of the customer and not of an exceptional nature in determining whether the amount was achieved or not (tenant aged over 70 years whose Annual income is less than one and a half times the annual amount of the SMIC art. 15-III of the Act of July 6 1989). "Consequently, it refused to recognize the significant liquidation of mutual funds. Supreme Court, 3rd Civil Chamber, decision of 28 May 1997.

1997. The relocation of the old tenant and low Income: judges do not have the substance to be seen whether the owner can legitimately claim the benefit of 15 Article III, paragraph 2 of the Act of 6 July 1989 especially because the lessor would own a another equivalent one. Supreme Court, 3rd Civil Case 8 July 1997.

1997. The estimated selling price of housing leaves when the law does not a market study or an expert to know the price of the property at sell. Court, Paris, 29 October 1997.

1997. Findings of the recovery period of a vacancy two years are fraudulent and cause damage and interests. Court, Paris, 14 October 1997.

1997. Leave disorders Neighborhood: disturbance both daytime and nighttime is a legitimate and serious non-renewal of the lease; the owner can serve a leave to the tenant for that reason. Court, Paris, 29 May 1997.

1997. Reality Check of the mutation with of employer: the owner is entitled to check with the employer, if necessary, the reality of mutation; investigations in this direction are in nothing-indelicate behavior of a fault. Court of Versailles, 5 December 1997.

1996. Takeover of housing by the owner for living, "the tenant cannot prevent the resumption of living accommodation provided for by Article 15-I of the Law 6 July 1989, arguing that the beneficiary of the recovery has alternative accommodation. »Indeed, it as the owner is free to settle in that it decides. «Court of Appeal of Nîmes 2 Chamber A, 5 December 1996.

1996. Relocation of housing during the period notice: housing may be held before the end of notice by another tenant. Therefore, the tenant maintains its replacement in agreement with the lessor and that this replacement takes effect before the expiry of notice. In this case the tenant which issued the leave, shall be liable in proportion to the period of occupation real housing. The obligation to pay rent and charges weigh on the new tenant "from that date. Supreme Court, 3rd Civil Case 12 June 1996.

1996. Point of the period of notice: a court of Appeal rightly held that the notice must be calculated from the date of delivery of the letter to recipient and not the date of its arrival at the office post. Supreme Court, 3rd Civil Case 10 January 1996.

1996. Referral to the Departmental Committee Conciliation is not envisaged by law, case of leave: Article 15 of the Act of 6 July 1989 the tenant does not challenge the reason for the leave enter the conciliation commission. Supreme Court, 3rd Civil Chamber, decision of 17 July 1996.

1996. The reason for serious and legitimate reason is the judge when it is invoked by the owner to give the tenant a Société civile immobilière (SCI) has notified its leave tenants citing the renovation of the building after lease, leading the improvement of the distribution places and comfort, the importance of the work was not compatible with the maintenance of a family with three children at a young age. The court found that the renovation the building was "a legitimate and serious." Court of Cassation, 3rd Civil Chamber, 7 February 1996.

1996. Late acceptance of the offer to sell the tenants who have ordered the owner to appear in the to reiterate the notary deed at a time ranging well beyond the date of expiry of statutory period, their accepting the offer of sale is null and void and are deprived of any security of tenure. Supreme Court, 3rd Civil Chamber, decision of 3 April 1996.

1996. Extending the concept of abandonment of domicile: the unexpected departure of the tenant and his hospitalization for a stay in a defined long-term care constitute an abandonment of domicile. Court of Appeal Nancy, 19 December 1996.

1995. Cancellation of leave by an SCI: the leave is to be canceled

when it emanates from an established between civil society part-
ners. Court of Cassation, 3rd Civil Chamber, decision of 8 November 1995.

1995. Distinction between abandonment of home and leave:
Article 14 of the Act of July 6 does not distinguish between
the de facto abandonment of housing and neglect by a legal
regular leave. Supreme Court, 3rd Civil Chamber, On 6 December   1995.

1995. The power of the court of implementing rules expulsion: in
refusing to grant time to the occupier whose expulsion has been
ordered court judges background have used the discretion they
under Articles 613 L -1 and L 613-2. Supreme Court, third Civil
Chamber, decision of 8 November 1995.

1994. Effective date of expulsion by the Ownership: the mere
fact that the owner did not to expel from the date of expiry the
time allowed by the judge to the tenant does not show he gave up
performing this removal. Court of Appeal Paris, 7 July 1994.

1994. Invalidity of fixed and signed off by the tenant: are void for
fraud in the law leave pre-signed by the tenants to escape the
restrictive laws aimed at successive protect the interests of tenants. . Supreme Court, 3rd Civil Chamber, 12 October 1994.

1994. Notification of leave by a letter acknowledgment: an appellate court had violated Article 669 of the Code of Civil Procedure,
stating valid leave granted by letter with advice of delivery as she
had found that the letter was not delivered to the recipient. Supreme Court, 3rd Civil Chamber, decision of 14 December 1994.

1994. Failure to comply with the deadline for signing the deed notary for the sale: the tenant has not complied the deadline for signature of the notary cannot blame the owner to have transferred
the property with a third party purchaser. Crown Court, Paris, 6
October 1994. 1994. The pattern of job loss does not to a profession: a doctor in Grenoble, is rent an apartment for professional
use and housing; declining business, it is forced to close his medi-
cal practice, but fortunately, is also time jobs in Paris, forced to
move in delay, it gives off to his owner with a notice reduced to
one month, as it believes authorized (Act of 6 July 1989). The
pending trial is due to tenant. The ruling cannot be subject to appeal, Due to the low amount of litigation, the owner is appealing
then appeal. The decision of the judges of the Supreme is clear:
"The loss of employment or transfer does not involve a professional activity. » Supreme Court, 3rd Civil Chamber, decision

of 16 March 1994.

1994. Indifference of the change in distance leave: the reduction of the notice period of leave to one month, due to changing professional is not conditioned to a certain geographic distance imposed the new occupation of the tenant. Supreme Court, 3rd Civil Chamber, decision of 20 July 1994.

1994. The connection of the Chamber rented to a bigger apartment: is not a legitimate reason; seriously the will of the owner to link the Chamber occupied by the tenant in an apartment of five Chambers which is adjacent. Court of Paris, 2 May 1994.

1994. The combination of two different patterns of leave prohibits the sale off to reserves in owner the benefit of a leave previously notified for recovery is nil. Court of Chartres, 29 March 1994.

1994. Suspension of deportation: Judge of enforcement may suspend an expulsion order, as a derogation of the right common, where provisional execution is not attached of right to the decision. Crown court, Quimper, 5 October 1994.

1993. The leave provided by the tenant on a date premature given leave for a date early is valid and its effect must be postponed, the day for which it should have been given, the tenant did not notify again. Supreme Court, 3rd Civil Division, Case 3 November 1993.

1993. Leave by the only Keys: according Article 12 and 15 of the Act of 6 July 1989, the tenant must send the owner a registered letter or notification by a bailiff. "The keys to the concierge and the telephone call from the tenant to the owner doe can be considered as a regular holiday. Supreme Court, 3rd Civil Chamber, decision of 24 March 1993.

1993. Conviction of the owner in case of fault leave the lessor may be sentenced to pay damages to the tenant for the costs incurred during the relocation and rehabilitation of his new apartment as compensation for its material damage resulting from the grant of leave illegal. Court of Besançon, 18 June 1993.

1992. The conditions of the offer to sell when the sale of housing to a third party does not give rise to more advantageous terms than those contained in the act of the offer had been made to the tenant, the notary was not obliged to make the notification of the sale. Supreme Court, 3rd Civil Chamber, decision of 12 February 1992.

1992. The internship does not qualify for notice reduced to one month: the court is that this is not a sufficient reason to qualify a reduced notice. Court of Saint-Girons, 9 January 1992. 1992. Leave validated only in cases of divorce pronounced: a husband who had granted leave to the lessor claimed on the basis of the Court of Cassation of 13 December 1989 (referred to below chronologically), be reached, the subsequent payment post rents owed by his wife. The court Cassation, in this case - October 13, 1992 - back in this case, thus confirming the decision of the Paris Court of Appeal in reaffirming that the spouses, accordance with Articles 220 and 262, Civil Code, are severally liable to the intervention a divorce decree issued regularly, debts for the maintenance of the household. Thus, despite the leave granted by the husband, it remains jointly and severally liable with his wife for payment of rent. Supreme Court, 3rd Civil Chamber, decision of 13 October 1992.

1992. Leave notified one of the spouses: the lessor had granted leave to sell only to Lessee of origin while the latter had married before the conclusion of the lease. The Paris Court of Appeal admits the regularity of such leave, dismissing the action for nullity introduced by the husband, on the basis Article 1751 of Civil Code, noting that he had during the signing of the lease, knowingly concealed the existence of his wife. The leave shall, in any event be issued to both spouses in separate letters. Shutdown mentioned does not question this principle but reduces the scope by requiring a minimum of good faith on the part of the original licensee. Court of Appeal of Paris, 6 the Chamber B, 16 March 1992.

1991. Profitable resale of a home purchased by the tenant is legal: no provision of the law the tenant does play to his right of preemption under the pretext that it will resell the property with a profit substantial provided there is no maneuver attention to this illegal law. Supreme Court, 3rd Chamber Civil Case 16 October 1991.

1991. Leave premature for sale by the Ownership: leave prematurely is deemed given take effect on the date for which it should have been given, so when the leave is based on the decision sell. The offer of the lessor is valid for both first months of the period of six months must be calculated backwards in time from the date expiry of the contract. High Court, Paris, 8 April 1991.

1990. There is no extension of preemption in the case of leave for sale: the deadline for two months granted by law the tenant to make its intention to exercise its right of preemption is not extended that it has expressed its intention to buy housing but at a price lower than the lessor proposed it. It may thus, after the period of two months, sell the apartment to a third recital that acceptance by the tenant on condition of price reduction did not amount to an acceptance of supply. Supreme Court, 3rd Civil Case 20 June 1990.

1990. Leave for loss of employment of the holder of the lease The job loss must affect the owner personally the lease and not the person living in the rented accommodation or guarantee. Supreme Court, 3rd Civil Chamber, 21 March 1990.

1990. Condition of termination of lease by a new buyer: the buyer cannot act on termination of lease for acts prior to his purchase, unless they have been validated specifically in the deed of sale. Indeed, the owner may take action against the tenant when the offense charged is continued after the sale. Supreme Court, 3rd Civil Chamber, 14 November 1990. 1989. Leave given to married couples awaiting divorce under section 1751 of the Civil Code "the right the lease of the space actually used for human habitation of the two spouses is deemed to belong to one and the other spouse ".

However, an appellate court, which stated that a husband a divorce was not required to jointly payment of rent, is legally justified its decision by holding that it had terminated the relationship between the owner and the tenant by sending a letter off. Court of Cassation, 3rd Civil Chamber, decision of 13 December 1989.

1987. Retraction of the tenant after giving his leave, leave, because of its unilateral nature, has not need to be accepted to be effective. An appellate court found that the shrinkage of the leave given by the Tenants of a flag had not been accepted by the lessor, has rightly held that it could not produce any effect and that they had become, by virtue this leave, squatters rights or title. Supreme Court, 3rd Civil Chamber, decision of 29 April 1987.

1987. Tenure after the deadline for notice: once the deadline expires the author leave the obligation to leave. If the latter, although the leave took effect, continues in places, it will be liable not rent but an allowance that the occupation judge may set a sum equivalent to the amount of rent. Moreover, his deportation may be ordered on the request of the lessor under an action for relief. Supreme Court, 3rd Civil Case April 29 1987.

CHAPTER II

RENTAL CHARGES

Most of the law

Article 23 of the Act of July 6 sets out the charges, in particular by reference to the list of components, which is determined by decree (list attached). Content of Article 23: charges recoverable amounts
ancillary to the main rent, payable on proof in return:
- 1 for services rendered related to the use of different elements of the rented property.
- 2 ° maintenance costs and small repairs on items of common use of the thing leased.
- 3 "of the annual representative lease law (Law No. 98-1267 of 30 December 1998, Article 12-j-II) and the corresponding charges for services which benefit the tenant. Note: the right to lease (2.5% excluding rent) is deleted for all tenants since 1 January 2001.
The list of these charges is fixed by Order in Council of State. The charges may give rise to the payment of provisions and, if so, to be adjustment at least annually. Applications provisions are justified by the communication of results earlier arrested in the previous regularization and when the property is subject to the status of the condominium or when the lessor is a corporation, by the budget estimates. A month before this correction, the lessor notify the tenant by the nature of breakdown charges and, in buildings, the method of distribution among the tenants. During a month of sending the figures, the supporting documents are required available to tenants.

Examples of case law

2000. Account of charges: are not justification under Article 23, paragraph 1 of the Act of 6 July 1989, the management accounts with no ventilation allows the tenant to verify the accuracy of recoverable expenses. Court of Appeal of Paris, 6 the Chamber B, 14 December 2000.

1999. Rent and charges, then the lease is considered verbal: the clause in a lease housing, providing a lump sum of rent and load distribution without distinguishing between the amounts payable in respect of rents and dues as charges and taxes, was declared non-written by the Court of Appeal Paris. Such a clause is contrary to Article 3 of the Act of 6 July 1989 imposing the amount of rent and Article 23 of the Act under which the charges are payable on vouchers. Judges of Appeal felt it is not necessary, however, to cancel the entire lease. Paris Court of Appeal, 6th Chamber B, 25 March 1999.

1999. Tenants should not bear amortization of heating: the Court of Appeal of Toulouse ruled, "the lessor who entrusts operation of heating to a company must ensure that it does not charge the tenants that are he would be entitled to recover if he ensured himself this benefit. » Court of Appeal of Toulouse, 3 rd Chamber 1st section, 16 March 1999.

1999. Costs of clearing garbage dump: giving an exhaustive list of charges recoverable in the Annex of the Decree of 26 August 987
the Supreme Court stated, "staff costs for the unblocking of the garbage dump requested by the donor should be excluded from the rent. » This list, in fact, refers to products and disinfecting columns garbage dump, but not personnel costs necessary to complete the transaction. Supreme Court, 3rd Civil Chamber, 10 March 1999.

1998. Condition to recover the TEOM (tax as garbage collection) on the tenant "did not justify the reality of the TEOM, the lessor of a building located in a municipality where the tax did not appear independently in the budget communal, for which no tax rate was established, and which gave rise to any product.» Municipalities have, indeed, the possibility of Tax support garbage collection by the municipal budget, in part fueled by the tax built on the properties, in which case the owner may not recover the fee for garbage removal in its tenant. Supreme Court, 3rd Civil Case 10 June 1998.

1997. The expenditure breakdown of the parties municipalities are not charges, is void any provision responsibility collective of tenants in case of deterioration of an element common of the leased property. Thus, charges campaigns-proof (including cleaning and painting) cannot be regarded as rent, or be passed, even partially, on the tenants. Supreme Court, 3 rd Civil Chamber, 17 July   1997.

1996. Reimbursement of expenses and prescription: a donor who had for six years set tax as garbage collection instead of his tenant was dismissed (as he referred to the prescription quinquennial enacted by section 2277 of the Civil Code) of request reimbursement from the latter on the ground "It belonged to the owner to justify each year its request under the fee for garbage removal household and a reminder of six years is not eligible. The Supreme Court ruling that breaks Whereas "in so doing, while loadings must be refunded on proof, the court proceedings violated the above texts. Supreme Court, 3 rd Civil Chamber, 3 April 1996.

1996. The expenses of renovation of the building do not constitute rent: indeed, the Decree of 6 August 1987 does not specify regarding the common external. But it follows of Article 1720 Civil Code that the lessor is required to deliver it in good repair of all kinds, therefore to make all necessary repairs other than leasehold during the lease term. Supreme Court of 3 rd, Civil Chamber, 21 February 1996.

1996. The binding and comprehensive list of recoverable expenses: legal provisions limiting the recoverable nature of the charges on the tenant have a mandatory; the parties have no right to waive, even in referring to the settlement of ownership. Court of Appeal of Aix-en-Provence, 18 December 1996.

1995. Disputed charges: no law or regulation prohibits tenants challenge before the limitation period, the amount of charges they feel they paid too. Court for instance, Paris, 12 October 1995.

1995. Expenses cleaning graffiti: the charges cleaning graffiti on interior walls as outside are not recoverable on the tenants, the Tenants are not responsible for damage Volunteers of others (Article 4-E of the Act of 6 July 1989). Paris Court of Appeal, 6th Chamber B, 12 May 1995.

1995. Tax sweeping sidewalks: the fee is recovered automatically by the owner on the tenant. Ministerial response, the official newspaper of the Assembly National, 18 September 1995. 1994. Method of load distribution: the distribution expenses can legally be done by the method of milliseconds based on the amount of space and utility from the facilities or services common. Court, Paris, 18 May 1994.

1994. The distinction between maintenance costs of other expenses "when the cleaning service the property is insured under a contract for and that the bills do not distinguish expenses recoverable from other expenditure, maintenance cannot be charged to the tenant. Supreme Court, 3 rd Civil Chamber, 5 October 1994. 1994. Rental of garbage: the cost of location of a trashcan, not specified in the list of Decree of 26 August 1987 establishing the list of charges recoverable, is not part of the latter. « Supreme Court, 3rd Civil Chamber, 5 October 1994.

1993. Mandatory loads utilities: the use or not the services collective, we are required to share expenses that correspond. This has been notified that a tenant refused to pay its expenses of heating on the ground it does not use it. Only people who live in ground floor are not required to participate in lift charges, unless it serves only the sub-soil. Court of Appeal of Reims, 1 July 1993. 1993. Justification of charges: the evidence of charges cover not only the nature and category loads but also on their distribution pattern between several units or tenants, egg in the case of water bills on behalf of the lessor that do no details on their mode of distribution, thus depriving tenants of any possibility of even they do not have access to the meter. Magistrates Court, 19 May 1993.

CHAPTER III

WORK OR IMPROVEMENT OF MAINTENANCE NEIGHBORHOOD AND DISORDERS

Most of the law

Articles 6 and 7 of the Act of 6 July 1989 and hangs introduced by the Act of 13 December 2000 codify the respective obligations of the tenant and the owner, in field of housing maintenance, repairs or processing and use peaceful places.

Article 6. "The owner is required to deliver to the tenant a housing leaving not show risk manifest prejudicial to the physical safety or to health and with the elements making it consistent with residential use. " The corresponding characteristics are defined by Order in Council of State for residential space primary or mixed-use in the first paragraph of Article 2 and premises referred to in the second paragraph of article, except for housing-homes that are subject to specific regulations (Law No. 2000-1208 of 13 December 2000, Article 187-II-2, known as the solidarity and Urban renewal - SRU).

The lessor is obliged:

- A) deliver to the tenant housing in good condition use and repair, as well as equipment mentioned in the lease in good condition operation, but the parties may agree in an express clause of the work that the tenant will perform or will be performed and the manner of their allocation on the rent, this clause provides for the duration of this allocation and, in case of early departure of the tenant, the terms of its compensation on proof of expenditure; such a clause may relate only to housing meet the minimum standards of comfort and livability defined by the decree mentioned in Article 25 of Law No. 86-1290 23 December 1986 to promote investment rental, home ownership housing and development of the supply of land;

- B) Ensure the tenant quiet enjoyment of housing and, without prejudice to Article 1721 Civil Code, to ensure defects or defects that would except to frustrate those recorded in the statement of places, would have been the subject of the clause expressly mentioned in subparagraph a above.

- C) To maintain the premises in condition to serve for the use under the contract and make all repairs, other than rent, required maintenance and to the normal maintenance of the leased premises.

- D) Not to oppose developments by the tenant, since they do not transformation of the rented property. Article 7.

The tenant is obliged:

- A) To pay the rent and expenses recoverable with the terms agreed the monthly payment is right when the tenant so requests.

- B) Peaceful use of leased premises after the destination that has been given the lease.

- C) Address of damage and losses occur during the term of the contract at the premises which it is exclusive, unless he proves they were held by force majeure, the fault of lessor or the act of a third party has not introduced into the housing.

- D) to cover the routine housing, equipment specified in the contract and minor repairs and all repairs leasehold defined by decree in Council of State, unless they are caused by outdated, defective, faulty construction, fortuitous event or force majeure.

- E) To let it perform in the leased premises Work to improve the common areas or parts deprivation of the same building, and the work necessary for the upkeep and maintenance of premises leased and the provisions of the second and third paragraphs of Article 1724 of the Civil Code are applicable to this work.

- F) not to convert the premises and equipment hired without the written consent of the owner (if this Agreement the latter may require the tenant of his departure scene) their surrender to the state or to retain the profit processing carried out without the tenant can claim compensation for expenses incurred. The lessor however, may require the tenant to surrender immediately places in the state where the transformations jeopardize the proper functioning of equipment or security of the premises.

- G) To insure against the risks which must respond as lessee and to justify at the Keys each year, at the request of the lessor. The rationale for this insurance resulting from delivery to lessor of a certificate from the insurer or its representative "(Act n ° 94-624 of 21 July 1994, Article 12).

Any clause providing for termination of right of contract lease for lack of insurance is effective only months after command remained unsuccessful. This commands again, on pain of nullity, the paragraph.

The termination of the contract: the law SRU (Solidarity and urban renewal) of 13 December 2000 requires, under penalty of inadmissibility of the application, notify the assignment termination in the "representative of the State" in department - in this case the prefect - the request is motivated by "a rental debt, the housing is subject to the Act of 6 July 1989. Prohibition to the tenant to have a dog dangerous in the slot it is allowed to the lessor to prohibit a dog from the first category in the housing - as defined by Article 3 of Law 6 January 1999, such an attack dog Pit bull, bull or Boer dog's appearance Mastiff or Tisa. Answer Ministerial Official Journal of 10 February 2003.

Examples of case law

2001. Noisy work: the development of an attic in habitable Chamber causes noises that exceed the usual drawbacks of the neighborhood. It is the duty of the author to create a device to mitigate significantly inconvenience suffered. Supreme Court, 3rd Civil Chamber, 28 February 2001.

2001. Work and termination clause in bad faith a tenant refuses to pay his rent because of local unhealthy and non-issuance of rent, by correcting itself, the lessor shall issue then payment order by invoking the termination clause. The tenant appeals in cassation court and the case decision of the judges of appeal and give due to the tenant. The Appeals judges should look to whether the lessor was not in bad faith, because each contractor has obligations. Supreme Court, 3 rd Civil Chamber, 3 April 2001.

2001. Partial reimbursement works: the customer may obtain a refund if there is a situation emergency and when the change was a result of in the most economical way possible. Thus, when another company could do work more cheaply, the reimbursement is not full. Supreme Court, 3rd Civil Chamber, decision of 12 June 2001.

2000. Special responsibility Chambermate: a tenant was found liable for abnormal disorder neighborhood when fed his pigeons on the balcony of his apartment so that we could not hold on terrace adjacent safely be sprayed by bird droppings. Court of Appeal of Paris, 8 the Chamber D, 10 February 2000.

2000. Obligation to protect windows: the owner was sentenced to ask protections bays windows when the tenant was the victim of several burglaries facilitated by the fact that the terrace housing has two windows with no protections. Court of Appeal of Rouen, Appeals Chamber priority, 21 March 2000.

2000. Tenant living loudly: the tenant receives in its housing noisy or visitors walking it with shoes with heels slams the door and moves the furniture does not require enjoyment of the premises. Court of Appeal of Dijon, 1st Chamber, 24 March 2000.

2000. Noises of domestic animals: the owner animals was sentenced to repair the damage suffered by its neighbors, following a detailed assessment of Usher attesting songs acute roosters, the gossip of ducks, turkeys and chortle cries of geese occur either simultaneously or alternately. Court of Appeal of Paris, 8 the Chamber a, 21 November 2000.

1999. Transformation of housing as a result of work to improve the tenant, without authorization, contrary to the terms of the lease, demolish a bulkhead and install a shower, have a committed offense serious enough to warrant termination of the location? "To the extent that such work had caused damage to housing or to the structure of the building and constitute the work of improvement, this issue is answered in the negative "(Article 6-d of the Act of 6 July 1989 prohibits the owner to oppose adjustments made by the lessee, since these do not convert the leased premises. The difficulty lies ultimately in the assessment of the concept of transformation and the consequences of the fault of the tenant in respect of the lease. Supreme Court, 3rd Civil Chamber, Case 13 July 1999.

1999. Loss of sunlight, in urban areas: it will be particularly difficult to see that the construction of a building at the edge of the property causes loss of sunlight as it is a disorder abnormal area. Supreme Court, 3rd Chamber civil, 14 December 1999. 1999. Upgrading of the electricity demand of Decree of 6 March 1987: in particular the owner must provide housing equipped with an electrical conform to standards. Court of Appeal of Paris, 6 the Chamber, 1 June 1999.

1999. Excessive barking dog is an abuse of enjoyment that the tenant left his dog to bark abnormally for several hours. Court of Appeal Paris, 6th Chamber B, 14 January 1999.

1999. Odors: odors due to the operation of an industrial poultry breeding, with effects on the health of neighbors, are a Neighborhood disorder that exceeds the disadvantages usually eligible. Supreme Court, 2nd Civil Chamber, 25 November 1999.

1999. Instances of non-repayment of work: "When the owner has not given its approval in writing the tenant cannot obtain such reimbursement if it has, previous owner put on notice to meet its obligation and was allowed in court to usurp the owner to carry out the work. » In the case before the Court of Appeal of Versailles, the tenants had decided only to change the boiler without sending consumption or a notice, in particular by a bailiff, to explicitly ask the owner change of the device, and without a judicial authorization - confirmation of a decision of the Supreme Court in 1996, cited below -. Court of Appeal Versailles, 1st Chamber, 19 November 1999. 1998. Terms of an agreement to work: the owner cannot afford to provide housing comply with the decree of 6 March 1987, the owner could not, for example, to charge, even by agreement, repairing the roof while, in fact, housing is not even living in the state. Court of Appeal of Dijon, 1st Chamber, 2 October 1998.

1997. Verify operation of heating during heating: the owner cannot oppose the tenant to have accepted the premises in the state where they found when the contract was signed in July when problems with heating and ventilation could not be detected. Court of Limoges, 1st April 1997.

1997. Why the tenant can stay the payment of rent? Only one disorder realization making places uninhabitable allows the tenant to suspend the payment of rent. The Court of Appeal refused this facility to tenants who reported disorders enjoyment resulting from the malfunctioning of the system sanitation resulting odor described by pestilential them to justify the interruption of payment their rent. Indeed, the tenants did not show that these disorders render the leased premises uninhabitable. Court of Appeal de Paris, 6 the Chamber, 25 November 1997.

1997. Illegal occupation of premises: the illegal occupation places cannot be a legitimate means of exerting pressure for implement the right to housing, the details of which are fixed by law. Court of Appeal de Paris, 14 the Chamber A, 26 November 1997.

1997. The aggressiveness of a dog is an abuse of enjoyment of the premises of an aggressive dog or his attitude threat to other tenants - case also judged in the same direction by the Court of Appeal of Paris, 13 February 1995 -. Court of Antony, 5 May 1997.

1997. Payment of rent to a notary in a case where rents had been paid by the lessee and entrusted to a notary, the lessor is entitled to rely on the termination clause of the lease for non-payment of rent. The Court decided in the affirmative: "The payment rent must be made to the creditor or someone who authority to or is authorized by the court or by law to receive him. » Because in this case, the notary, in which the payments were made, was no longer the representative of lessor. The tenant knew, which does not allow it to invoke any apparent mandate. Supreme Court, 3rd Civil Chamber, 5 March 1997.

1997. Water heater and boiler defective housing cannot be considered in good working condition to the entry of the customer, in accordance with the decree of March 6 1987, when the water heater and boiler are defective. Court of Appeal of Aix-en-Provence 1st Chamber A, 18 June 1997.

1997. Non-renewal of the lease of a noisy tenant the Paris Court of Appeal approved the no prolongation, the lease of a tenant who was engaged to an uproar both daytime and night-time in the circumstances follows: seven of his neighbors were bothered by noise generated by the tenant, who, when returning in the evening due of his profession, did not take all precautions and to peacefully enjoy the property leased, and received particularly noisy friends and listening to music late into the evening. Yet the owner and the trustee to had sent a letter stating that making the noise, it disturbed the peace of its neighbors. According to the court, "This apparent lack of care was a matter legitimate and serious non-renewal of the lease. » Court of Appeal de Paris, 8 the Chamber B, 29 May 1997.

1996. Work performed by the tenant to remedy deficiencies of the owner: the tenant can obtain reimbursement of costs incurred to remedy the lack of maintenance of the owner if he has not obtained prior court permission to enter these costs. Supreme Court, 3rd Civil Case 10 July 1996.

1996. Work of the floor and the door-window housing at the expense of the owner: the judges held that the owner has to repair the floor and the door of the housing can damage are not attributable to the tenant. Court of Privas, 7 February 1995 and Paris, 3 April 1996.

1996. The concept of age: after recalling that "Only should be charged to tenant damage caused by the mere fact, except for those caused by age, the court of Puteaux said it is customary to set five years the average occupation beyond which the rehabilitation and renewal must be regarded as inherent in wear places and equipment and, as such, incurred by the lessor alone. «Court of Puteaux, 1 October 1996.

1996. Cases of violence against the tenant's keeper: If the tenant of violence against the guard the building, the lessor is entitled to terminate the lease without to give notice to the tenant to use peaceful places leased. Court, Paris, 7 November 1996.

1996. Noise in the building work "has violated the principle that no person shall cause a disturbance to others abnormal Neighborhood court of appeal which, to dismiss a Syndic of joint ownership of his claims pursuant to work of compliance of a lot to be leased and damages - interest for noise pollution, has attracted that this work was the responsibility of the tenant, who had been warned to stop this nuisance, while the victim of a neighborhood trouble finding his origin in the building let may seek compensation from the owner. " Supreme Court, 3rd Civil Chamber, 17 April 1996.

1995. Work necessary for the survival of equipment when the heating is insufficient to point affect the habitability of housing, the lessor shall to repair other than leasehold. The quality of lessor, the rent is, in these circumstances indifferent. Supreme Court, 3rd Civil Division, 5 July 1995.

1995. Limits of the prohibition of the owner to the processing premises by the tenant: work painting and laying carpet made by the tenant are mere accommodations. Similarly it cannot be accused of having the tenant chose colors current when these colors are not Eccentric and do not prevent the habitability of the premises by originality. In addition, we cannot blame the tenant not painted white housing as it was origin. Court of Nancy, February 1st Case 1995.

1995. The rehabilitation of the electricity load owner: the rehabilitation of the electrical installation not under the tenant's repairs, it must be charged to the owner. Court for instance, Paris, 11 October 1995.

1995. Grounds for suspension of the rent for no habitability of the apartment in case of impossibility living housing the licensee may properly refuse to pay the rent. Court of Appeal de Nancy, 2 Chamber, 12 September 1995.

1995. Application of the Decree of 6 March 1987 on living standards even if the housing need not be given to new, it requires that the state allows it decent living, the Order of March 6 must therefore 1994. Improvement works and digital code: Installation a digital code can be a definite improvement. Court of Appeal de Paris, 16 September 1996.

1994. Dog bite: is a major disorder Neighborhood bite of a German shepherd, despite warnings to the tenant who remained at liberty and unattended. Court of Appeal of Dijon, 14 April 1994.

1993. Improvement works that may be taken into account when renewing the lease: the improvement work and repairs which the owner is obliged, under Article 6-c of the Act of 6 July 1989 can not constitute work for improvement in the part of the decree limiting rents in metropolitan Paris, under Article 18 of the Act. Thus the work of cleaning the walls, sealing gable walls are maintenance work preserving the heavy lifting, so the modification of existing green spaces and the replacement Rescue blocks do not work improvement. Court, Paris, November 8 1993.

1993. The obligation to ensure the functioning of heating to the owner: the owner cannot evade the obligation to ensure operation of heating and electrical installation and the closed and covered to prevent infiltration. Supreme Court, 3 rd Civil Chamber, decision of 27 January 1993.

1993 owner's obligation to deliver a housing in good working condition: the tenant cannot be turned down his request for reimbursement work and rents on the grounds that he knew perfectly what state were the leased premises and that the repairs he did have to stay at his office according to its commitments, without being sought, as asked if the homes had been issued in good condition use and repair, if the equipment rental were in good working condition and if a clause express the work to put the burden of the tenant and specified the procedure for charging on the rents. Supreme Court, 3rd Civil Chamber, decision of 7 July 1993.

1992. Compensation for work: when tenants are either forced to leave, is required to use a heating because of defects thermal insulation, the owner is condemned to compensate for additional equipment and energy consumption. Supreme Court, 3rd Civil Division, 3 June 1992.

1991. Allocation of work to improve the cost of work performed in common areas must be divided by the number of dwellings owned by the owner. Court, Paris, 25 June 1991.

1991. Noise pipe in the building: a couple Tenants no longer support the noise caused by night suppressers water their building located in Issy-les - Moulineaux. On 7 March 1990, the Court of Appeal of Versailles accepted the responsibility of the owner SCI. SCI is then provides for judicial review - the intensity of the noise under investigation being lower than the limits of regulation 1969 and 1978 - the Court rules: "The owner is required law to ensure the tenant quiet enjoyment. Since these sounds, because of their frequency, their limit the emergence and characteristics tyrannical, cause a disturbance to tenants of enjoyment, they are entitled to compensation for the damage they have suffered. "Supreme Court, 3rd Civil Chamber, Case 4 December 1991.

1990. Termination of lease for damage done to a tenant neighbor: the termination of a lease has been justified by the Paris Court of Appeal that the son of a tenant had violated the safety of neighbors, including one victim was shot by a gun in the window of his apartment and stone in the window. Court of Appeal of Nîmes, 13 December 1990.

1990. Repair of fire damage to the policyholder is obligated to repair all the damage caused to owner because of the fire caused by him. There is no appropriate to make a deduction for obsolescence. Supreme Court, 3rd Civil Chamber, 9 January 1990.

1990. Installation of the components of security: the owner did not ensure the tenant's enjoyment disorder caused by third parties, including through votes of fact. It was therefore not required pose components to avoid potential robberies and improve safety. Supreme Court, 3rd Chamber Civil, 15 April 1990.

1990. Responsibility of the owner: the Lessor is responsible for the assault made possible by its personal or a lack of supervision of those who represent. It is responsible for theft fostered by scaffolding supported the house for its renovation. Supreme Court, 3rd Civil Chamber, 28 February 1990.

1987. The possession of many animals constitutes a domestic disturbance near the tenant who has eleven dogs and four cats had violated Article 7 of the Act of 6 July 1989 requiring the use peaceful places. Court of Appeal of Aix-en-Provence, 22 December 1987.

CHAPTER IV

STATE OF THE DEPOSIT FILING GUARANTEE AND BONDING

Most of the law

The refund of the security paid by the tenant on arrival in the housing and the conditions bonding, are sources of many disputes. Article 22 of the Act of 6 July 1989 and the new Article 22-1 of the Law 21 July 1994 set out the rules.

Article 22. When a deposit is required under the rental contract to secure fulfillment of obligations rental of the tenant, it cannot exceed two month's rent in principal (excluding rent expense). A deposit can be expected when the rent is payable in advance for a period exceeding two months; however, if the tenant is claiming the benefit payment Monthly rent, pursuant to Article 7 the lessor may require a security deposit. It is returned within a maximum period of two months from the return of the keys by the tenant, less the Where appropriate, the amount outstanding to the lessor and sums, which it might be, instead of tenant, provided they are duly justified. The amount of this deposit is non-interest bearing, at benefit of the tenant. There must be no revision during the execution of the lease, possibly renewed.

A failure to return within the prescribed period, the balance of deposit guarantee outstanding tenant after arrested accounts, product interest at the statutory rate to the tenant. Article 22-1. "When the bond obligation resulting from a lease entered into under This title contains no indication of duration or when the length of guarantee is provided indefinite, the guarantor may terminate it unilaterally. The Termination shall take effect at the end of the lease, it as the

41

original contract or a contract or extended renewed. The person standing surety preceded his signature the reproduction of the handwritten amount of rent and conditions for its review as set out in contract location of the hand in expressing explicit and unequivocal knowledge of it nature and extent of the obligation it contracted and handwritten reproduction of the preceding paragraph. The lessor gives the bond a copy of the lease. These formalities are prescribed on pain of nullity of bond (Law No 94-624 of 21 July 1994, Article 23 -I).

Examples of case law

2001. Restraint condition of the deposit: "End of lease, the owner claiming damage committed by the tenant to withhold all or a part of the deposit is not required to produce bills paid work. » According to this view the only the owner has a legal obligation towards the tenant to justify the amount of damages claimed. However, it is not obliged to carry out rehabilitation. A quote from a professional, example could be sufficient to establish the amount of repairs. Of course, the tenant retains the possibility of challenge the amount of the estimate if he considers overvalued. Supreme Court, 3rd Civil Chamber, decision of 3 April 2001.

2000. The default state of affairs: the judge cannot reject the presumption that the tenant has received local rented in good condition to specify whether the lessor hindered the establishment of the state of play. Supreme Court, 3rd Civil Chamber, decision of 16 May 2000.

2000. The removal of garbage dump: the owner can delete, without reducing the rent, provided garbage dump the lease when its decision is based on a legitimate and seriously, the equipment had been declared in a state not comply with hygiene. Supreme Court, 3rd Chamber Civil Case 2 February 2000.

1999. The principle of caution: nothing in the Act of 6 July 1989 prohibits the owner to require a personal bond or bank. Court, Paris, 18 February 1999.

1999. The age of the electrical installation: the owner must issue a housing suitable for living (Article 6 the Law of 6 July 1989, Decree of 6 March 1987 laying down minimum conditions of comfort and since 30 June 2002 Decree on the housing), "the release, by the owner, an apartment equipped with inadequate power to normal requirements and security constitutes a failure to issue. This generator is unsuitable for the tenant, a prejudice resulting from the decreased use of the apartment. « Court of Appeal of Paris, 6 the Section C Chamber, 1 June 1999.

1999. Impact on the lease termination bond: the release of the bond which does at the end of the initial lease or contract may be renewed constitute a legitimate reason to leave serious condition that the tenant has agreed in the lease, the obligation express to maintain or renew the bond in case of termination. Court of Appeal of Paris, 6 the Chamber B, 14 January 1999.

1999. The establishment of a state of understanding between the parties is a free act: a state of the deposit contradictorily established between the parties or their representatives, such as real estate agent representing the owner does not give rise to compensation. No response Ministerial 2463, Official Journal of the National Assembly, 13 May 1999.

1999. Guarantor's: according to the Supreme Court, "in case of guarantee the execution of a residential lease and in the absence of any mention in providing the guarantee extension of the guarantor's obligations under the lease tacitly renewed or extended then the commitment is limited to obligations under the original lease.» The extension a guarantee or renewed lease must tacitly therefore be express. For example, we can draw on expression, already validated by an appeals court of Paris (see below, 7 July 1992): "This commitment will be valid until the expiry of the obligations of the tenant; his lease may be renewed by tacit agreement, legally or conventionally. Court of Appeal of Versailles, 1st Chamber B, 25 June 1999.

1999. The bank guarantee is allowed: a guarantor the effect of ensuring the payment of rents to come by availability of funds to the bank, so the clause of the lease requiring the tenant to provide security banking is allowed by the courts, the Court of Appeal Paris has acknowledged the validity. Court of Appeal of Paris, 6 the Chamber B, 18 February 1999.

1999. Caution in case of change of ownership: in the sale of housing, the deposit does not guarantee automatically the new lessor. requires that the tenant express its willingness to extend the guarantee to new owner. Supreme Court, 3rd Chamber civil, 26 October 1999.

1999. Caution unspecified time: if bond of indefinite duration, it was thought that because they unilaterally terminated his employment, the security is committed during the tacit agreement. Court for instance, Paris, 29 January 1999.

1998. Refusal to tenant participation in the statement of places of exit: an evaluation of output, although not contradictory, is enforceable against the tenant because of its own refusal to attend, found on site by the bailiff. Court of Aix-en-Provence, 26 February 1998.

1997. The proof of the claim of the owner: the absence of establishing an inventory, even of Because of the failure of the tenant is not sufficient to establish the claim of the lessor. Supreme Court, 3rd Civil Chamber, Case 8 January 1997.

1996. Evidence of deterioration of the tenant: Well and non-contradictory, the finding made by the bailiff deterioration caused by the tenant must be admitted as evidence, when it was realized immediately after the departure of the tenant, which did warned that subsequent owners. Supreme Court, 3 rd Civil Chamber, decision of 2 October 1996.

1996. Bad writing of the amount of the sum guaranteed by the bond: the bond is irregular and therefore has no effect if the amount warranty contained only digits or letters. Supreme Court, 1st Civil Chamber, 13 November 1996.

1996. Validity of the bond mentioned in pencil paper: the term of the tenant referred to in pencil does not the guarantor's undertaking, since using the pencil in the drafting of an act is under private defended by any text. Supreme Court, 8 October 1996.

1995. Rejection of the establishment of status by Usher: in the absence of any dispute relating to the status quo, the request for appointment of a bailiff, to proceed with the status quo must be rejected. Court of Clermont Ferrand, 30 November 1995.

1995. Poor understanding of the commitment of bond: Bonds which poorly control the French cannot rely on the misunderstanding of the language escape the consequences of his appointment because she signed. Court of Appeal in Chambéry, November 28 1995.

1995. Current situation and conditions of repair damage when he leaves the housing, the tenant is required to return in the condition stated on the document arrival. If no observation was included in the statement of points of entry, which is developed at the exit should not call any particular comment, except to demonstrate that the observed disorder is due to outdated or force majeure, the tenant is only required to make own accommodation and equipment in good condition operation. Supreme Court, 3rd Chamber Civil Case 20 December 1995.

1994. Notion of normal wear and tear of equipment there a limit on repairs, required of the tenant, because the lessor cannot require the replacement pure and simple a range of ten years old or coating it posed fourteen years ago, items damaged as a result of normal use of the dwelling. Court of Appeal of Besançon, 7 September 1994.

1994. Invalidity of a state of late: a report bailiff established more than three months after the departure of tenants lose any probative value and does not to attribute the work to tenants due to the Late of the operation. Court, Paris, March 11 1994.

1994. The deposit is Community contractors: it is wrong that an owner refuses to return the tenant the security deposit, claiming he had been paid by the husband before divorce, when in reality it this is a payment from the community and now belongs to one and the other spouse. Court for instance, Paris, 18 October 1994.

1993. The costs of setting up state of affairs are the entire burden of Usher: the direct use by bailiff a summons to attend a finding of state places is an unnecessary act which the bailiff has to bear the charge under Article 645 of the new code Civil Procedure. Supreme Court, 1st Civil Chamber, Case 17 November 1993.

1992. Limit the initiation of bond for an initial lease term to be determined: the owner-lessor sued the surety for failure to pay rent and accessories by the main tenant, while the duration of original lease - 6 years - had expired. The Court of Appeal Paris rejects her request noting, "the commitment bail had been given for the initial term of the lease and failing that, at the expiration of the contract, obtained from the Manager a new commitment, it could not be sought payment for rent and are materials relating to the period after. In analyzed the hypothesis that the duration of the commitment bond is not specified, the contract of guarantee is the enhancement of the lease, it cannot exceed the main contract. Thus, when the lease be extended or renewed, the deposit is more committed unless it has reiterated its warranty. Court of Appeal Paris, 8th Chamber A, 7 July 1992.

1990. Solidarity Chamber mates and return of deposit: the return of security deposit shall take place no later than two months after the departure of tenant, subject to the accounts that can follow. Since it serves to guarantee the performance, the tenant of its obligations, it cannot be returned before release of the premises. Thus, according to the Supreme Court when one of his Chamber mates gives leave under lease, it may require the owner to return his quote part of the deposit. He must wait until its tenants have vacated the scene to claim their share. Supreme Court, 3rd Civil Case 21 November 1990.

1990. At what point can we stop the undertaking of bail? By a decree of 25 April 1990, the Supreme Court annulled a decision by the court of the 20th district which had ordered the bond to pay the sums due from the tenant, although the bond is terminated prior to its commitment. The court of first instance had, in fact, considered that although a commitment of securities can be revoked on signing a new lease, it could not however be under lease. The Supreme Court holds, however, the indeterminate nature of lease that allows the bond to end any time his appointment. In these circumstances, implementation a commitment to guarantee may be extremely delicate and it is prudent to have against any challenge to the document signed by repeating it upon renewal of the lease. Supreme Court, 3 rd Civil Case April 25 1990.

1983. The amount of the deposit is not revision: the amount of the deposit may be subject to any revision, either during the contract or at renewal and practices that do not these provisions may result in civil penalties. Answer ministerial debates in 1982 and Assembly national in 1983.

CHAPTER V

CONTRACT RENEWAL AND SETTING AND EVOLUTION OF RENT

Most of the law

Chapter II of the Act of July 6 sets the duration of the contract, his sustainability mechanisms for renewal and modalities for the establishment or development of the rent and expenses. The duration of the contract Article 10. The rental contract is concluded for a period at least three years for those donors physical as well as donors defined in Article 13 and six years for corporate donors: "If the owner does not leave the formal requirements and time limits laid down in Article 15, the lease came to an end is to be renewed tacitly renewed. In case of automatic renewal, the contract period renewed for three years for those donors physical as well as donors defined in Article 13 and six years for corporate donors (Law No. 94 -- 64, 21 July 1994, Article 14-I). "In case of renewal, the contract period renewed at least equal to that defined in the first paragraph of this article "(Law No. 94-64 of 21 July 1994 Article 14-II). The offer of renewal is filed within the formal requirements and time limits provided for leave Article 15. The rent for the renewed contract is defined as rules laid down in Article 17-c of the Act of 6 July 1989.

Article 11. When a specific event that justifies the lessor natural person to take the Chamber for reasons professional or family, the parties may conclude a contract for less than three years but not less than one year. The contract must state the reasons and the event law: Notwithstanding the conditions of time under Article 15 confirms the lessor at least two months before term of the contract, the completion of the event. At the same time, the lessor may offer the report of the term of the contract if the performance of the event was postponed. He cannot use this option only once. When the incident occurred and is confirmed, the tenant is deprived of any right under occupation from the local to the term provided in the contract. When the event did not occur or is not confirmed, the lease is deemed to be three years. If the contract under this section follows a lease with the tenant for the same compartment, the rent may not exceed that of the former may be revised in accordance with second paragraph of Article 17-d of the Act of 6 July 1989. Article 11-1. "When a holiday for sale conform to provisions of Article 15 shall be issued by a relevant owner rental sectors defined in the fourth and fifth subparagraphs of Article 41 ter of Law No. 86-1290 of 23 December 1986, as part of a sale by lots more than ten houses in the same building, the lease may be expressly renewed for a shorter period to that provided by Article 10. The renewal of the lease shall be made in writing between the parties no later than four months before the expiration of the lease. At the end of the period fixed by the parties to the lease renewed, it shall be automatically terminated "(Law No. 2000-1208 13 December 2000, Article 198). Voluntary termination of the contract Article 12. The tenant may terminate at any time, in with formal requirements and time specified in the second paragraph of paragraph I of Article 15.

Article 13. The provisions of Article 11 and Article 15 can be invoked:

- A) When the lessor is a civil society exclusively between relatives and allies to fourth degree by the company included the benefit of one of associates.

- B) Where the accommodation is in possession, by any member of the possession. Abandonment of residence or death of the original tenant.

Article 14: In case of abandonment of domicile by the tenant, the lease continues:

- To the spouse without prejudice to Article 1751 Civil Code;
- The benefit of descendants who lived with him for at least one year the date of abandonment of the home;

- For the benefit of the partner related to the tenant through a pact registered partnership;
-    The   benefit   of   the   ascending   partner   known   or dependents, which lived with him since at least one year from the date of abandonment of domicile upon the death of the tenant, the lease is transferred:
- Without prejudice to the sixth and seventh paragraphs of Article 832 of the Civil Code to the surviving spouse;
- Descendants who lived with him for at least one year from the date of death;
- Partner-related tenant in a civil solidarity;
- Descendants, known to the partner or dependents that lived with him   for   at   least   one   year   from   the   date   of   death. In case of multiple applications, the judge decides in based on interests.
If persons who meet the requirements in this Article, the lease is terminated automatically law by the death of the tenant or the abandonment of the home by the latter. Rent increase upon renewal of the lease Article 17-c. When renewing the contract, the rent would leads to reassessment if it is clearly under evaluation. In this case, the lessor may offer the tenant at least six months before the term of the contract and conditions of form provided for in Article 15, a new rent set by references to rents usually found in the neighborhood for comparable housing in the conditions laid down in Article 19. When the owner applied the provisions of this c, it cannot give the tenant for same term. Notification reproduced, under penalty of nullity, the provisions of paragraphs c and the previous mentioned amount of rent and the list of references used to be determined. In case of disagreement or lack of response from the tenant four months before the term of the contract, either parties before the commission. In the absence of agreement found by the commission, the judge is prior to the term of the contract. If referral, the contract continued automatically with the conditions previous rent possibly revised. A contract, which the rent shall be deemed judicially, extended for the period defined in Article 10, from the date of expiry Contract. The judge's decision is provisionally enforceable. The increase agreed between the parties or determined to be judicially applies third or sixth depending on the length of the contract. However, this increase applies to the sixth annual contract renewed, then at the subsequent renewal once if it exceeds 10% if the first renewal had less than six years. The resulting revision of the below

applies to each value thus defined. Annual review of rent by the cost of Construction published by the INSEE Article 17-d: When the lease provides for the rent review, which occurs each year on the date agreed between the parties or, failing that, at the end of each year.

The rent increase that results cannot exceed "the variation of the average over four quarters of the index construction costs published by the INSEE (Law No. 94-624 of 21 July 1994, Article 17-I) measuring the cost of Construction published by the National Institute of Statistics and economic studies. If clause fixing the date, that date is the last index published at the date of signing of the lease. "The average above is the index of construction cost at the reference date and indices 68 three preceding quarters (Law No. 94-624 of 21 July 1994, Article 17-II).

The payment order in case of refusal by the tenant to meet the payments of rents or charges Article 24. Any clause providing for termination of right the lease for non-payment of rent or charges or agreed to terms for non-payment of the security deposit is effective only two months after a payment order remained unsuccessful: "A penalty of inadmissibility of the application, assignment for finding the termination shall be notified at the instance of the bailiff to the representative of the State in the department by registered letter with application accused of receiving at least two months before the hearing so that he understands, as necessary, bodies of the household, the Fund Solidarity for housing or social services competent.

The judge may, even ex officio, grant deadlines payments in accordance with Articles 1244-1, paragraph 1 and 1244-2 of the Civil Code, the tenant in a situation of settle its debt rental "(Law No 98-657 of 29 July 1998 Article 114-1 °).

During the course of time thus granted, the effects of termination clause are automatically suspended; these time and terms of payment granted might not affect the execution of the lease particularly suspend the payment of rent and expenses.

If the tenant is released from his debt within the time frame and in the procedures laid down by the judge, the termination clause of full right is deemed not to have played, in the case, it takes full effect. Command payment again, barely invalid, the provisions of the preceding paragraphs "and the first paragraph of Article 6 of Law No 90-449 of 30 May 1990 to the implementation of the right to housing, mentioning the option for the tenant to enter the Fund solidarity housing "(Law No 90-449 of 31 May 1990 Article 27) "whose address is specified (Law No 98-667 of 29 July 1998, Article 114-2).

"When the obligations of a lease concluded under this title are guaranteed by a bond, the payment order is served on the bond within 15 days from the significance of the tenant command. Otherwise, the deposit may be required to pay penalties or default interest "(Act n ° 94-624 of 21 July 1994, Article 24).

"The second subparagraph shall apply to assignments leading to the delivery of the termination of the lease when motivated by the existence of a debt of rent lessee (law n ° 2000-1208 of 13 December 2000, Article 188-3 °).

The collective settlement of disputes by delegation Article 24-1. "When one or more tenants with the same owner renting a dispute with a common origin, they may give a written mandate to sue them name and on behalf of an association serving the National Consultative Committee and approved for this purpose;

if the dispute concerns the characteristics of housing mentioned the first and second paragraphs of Article 6 this may also be given to an association of advocacy for people suffering exclusion by the accommodation referred to in Article 31 of Law No 98-657 of 29 July 1998 guidance on the fight against the exclusions and approved for this purpose. The provisions of the preceding paragraph shall apply to tenants of the premises mentioned in the second paragraph of Article 2 when the dispute relates to the rental of decency housing "(Act n ° 2000-1208 of 13 December 2000, Article 187-II-4).

Examples of case law

2002. Deadline for submission to the Departmental Committee Conciliation: there is no deadline for bringing of the commission. any referral is valid provided intervene before the expiry of the lease. Supreme Court, 3rd Civil Chamber, decision of 27 November 2002.

2002. The internal housing is not part of characteristics required for the references of rent: the provisions of the Decree of 31 August 1990 pursuant to Article 19 of the Act of 6 July 1989 do not mention the state inside the housing (state of repair or age of housing). Supreme Court, 3rd Civil Case 27 November 2002.

2002. The work done by the tenant cannot subtract the slot of the release of the 1948 Act: "Even if the work done by the tenant have to upgrade the housing of Class III to II B - one of prerequisites out of the Act of 1948 - the tenant can argue that fact to prevent the exit procedure of the law by an 8-year lease.»

2001. Transfer of lease on death of tenant regardless of the rental arrears - if the heirs waive inheritance - an owner recognizes the right to transfer the lease to the recipient fulfilling the conditions laid down by Article 14 of the Act of 6 July 1989 (including the recipient with lived for at least 1 year before the death of the original licensee) but contends that the waiver made by the person to succession of his mother, in this case was found destroyed by the application of benefit transfer of the right the lease and that it will also transfer initial obligations, inter alia, payment of rent Unpaid and justify its request to terminate the lease. The trial judge noted the independence of the right to transfer provided by law the right of acceptance or renunciation the succession. The Court of Appeal upheld that decision: the owner could not condition the transfer of the lease payment of rental arrears prior to death, the beneficiary or to renounce his inheritance. Court of Appeal Paris, 6th Chamber C, 4 April 2001.

2001. Refusal of issue of receipt by the owner followed the termination of the lease: the Court of Cassation held that the tenant could not criticize the owner non-issuance of receipts since it not paid on time and the rental terms that it also had an amount corresponding to 1-year rents. Supreme Court, 3 rd Civil Case 12 June 2001.

2000. Transfer of lease on death of tenant regardless of the rental arrears - if the heirs do not abandon the legacy - if, if death of the lessee, under Article 14 of the Act of 6 July 1989 provides for the automatic transfer of the lease for the benefit of certain people, it does not provide for recovery of arrears of rent deceased by the transferee. Noting that beneficiaries of the transfer of the lease had not commitment to pay the rental arrears, an appellate court to chosen, rightly, that no new tenants could be, as such, recognized debtors Arrears of rent and that, as heirs, they could not be condemned jointly and severally to pay that debt. The lessor should, in fact, to separately heirs who do not renounce the succession. Supreme Court, 3rd Civil Chamber, decision of 16 February 2000.

2000. Notification by a single letter recommended for both spouses: that the owner intends notify an offer of lease renewal or a husband to leave, must notify each of its intentions of both spouses by letters with AR distinct. The Supreme Court has to temper the rigor this requirement by accepting the validity of a proposal new lease made pursuant to Article 28 of the Act of 23 December 1986 (Article 28 allows for a proposal for release of the 1948 Act), notified by a single letter to the spouses co-owners of the lease, the ground that the notice of receipt of the letter was signed by each of the two spouses. This decision, of course, does not include donors to continue to notify their intentions by separate letters to tenants married. Supreme Court, 3rd Civil Chamber, Case 2 February 2000. 2000. Regularization of the lease record: the owner can apply for regularization of the lease even if the record occupied housing does not meet the standards of comfort and habitability of the Decree of 6 March 19987. Supreme Court, 3rd Civil Chamber, 29 October 2000.

2000. A definition of rent clearly undervalued : Rent clearly is under-appreciated function of the average rents in the neighborhood. Court of Appeal of Paris, 6 the Chamber B, 7 September 2000.

1999. The transfer of the lease in case of death of Tenant: Article 14 of the Act of 6 July 1989 allows the transfer housing to the surviving spouse as well as people who experienced at least one year with the tenant. The Supreme Court has held on an appellate court need to meet this minimum period of one year, in a case between the sons of the deceased to the lessor, the son who lived less than a year with her mother. Supreme Court, 3 rd Civil Case 13 July 1999.

1999. Abandoned homes and payment of rent: the tenant abandons the premises cannot rely on Article 14 of the Act of 6 July 1989 to be eligible freed from the payment of rent. "Whereas the of Article 14 of the Act of 6 July 1989 had no effect to defeat the treaty but to protect the partner or dependents abandoned where they were not Contracting personally. Court of Appeal of Rouen, 15 December 1999.

1999. Release of the 1948 Act: in addition to the requirements of income tenant, the judge must find that the premises are classified under Category II-B or II C in order to legitimize the offer to enter into a lease for eight years. Supreme Court, 3rd Civil Chamber, 3 February   1999.

1999. Verbal lease and leave the validity of the leave is not subject to the prior signature of a written contract, which the effective date will be its regularization; the owner may give leave upon the expiry of the lease record. Supreme Court, 3rd Civil Chamber, 27 January 1999.

1998. Decommissioning of a dwelling under the 1948 Act: housing should be classified in Class II when its characteristics are consistent with this category, when although it has no toilet or shower room or bathroom. Supreme Court, 3rd Civil Chamber, 4 November 1998.

1998. Use of the premises in the case of a lease mixed if the holder of the lease mixed-use professional and home is not required during the lease, to use the site to each use by agreement of the parties, it may not, when at the end of contract, it is not his principal residence for at least partially, taken into the premises location, rely the right to renew the contract under the law of 6 July 1989 to those who live in rented premises. Supreme Court, 3rd Civil Chamber, decision of 2 December 1998.

1998. Termination of lease for non-payment of rent: the owner can terminate the lease for a legitimate reason and serious, "including the failure by the tenant one of its obligations. » Failure to pay rent is such a serious and legitimate reason. Supreme Court, 3rd Civil Chamber, decision of 21 December 1998.

1998. Rejection references without reference to Street numbers: references rent that do not include at least ten numbers of the street where buildings are located are not admissible. Supreme Court, 3rd Civil Chamber, decision of 1 July 1998.

1998. Characteristics of references rent a rental housing "clearly under-valued" allows the donor-agency to propose at the renewal of lease, a new rent to the tenant by producing rent references usually found in the neighborhood; these should include, for each housing rent is given as a reference, the criteria set by Article 1 of the Decree of 31 August 1990. In a case where the owner only indicated for each reference, the area of housing, the entry of tenant and the current rent per square meter, the invalidity of the proposed new rent was imposed. According to judges and the references provided are inadequate "In these conditions the omissions had caused a grievance to tenants who were unable to verify either the reality or the comparability of the references on which the lessor had based its proposal to increase ". Court of Appeal Versailles, 1st Chamber B, 23 January 1998.

1998. Qualification of bail furnished: a furnished studio only a table and a cupboard, with the exception of a bed, cannot be regarded as rented furnished. Magistrates Court of Orleans, 29 June 1998.

1998. Furnished rental concept: the affirmation of furnished is not sufficient to prove the character furnished when the furniture rented with the premises are not quantity and quality sufficient to allow the tenant of living. Court of Rennes, 5 March 1998.

1998. The references must concern housing status: are not valid for references to non-approved housing while the revaluation of rent on a house door belonging to the sector agreement. Magistrates Court Versailles, 29 May 1998.

1998. Date of referral to the court prior to the notice delivery of the Departmental Committee Conciliation: the fact that the date of the summons in courts either prior to the opinion of the Divisional conciliation cannot affect the validity of this act that must occur before the maturity date of the lease, this that is the case. Court, Paris, 17 March 1998.

1998. Change of address of owner: the Tenant shall not suffer the consequences of failure of his owner who failed to share his change of address, which is the requirement for the requirement under Article 3 of the Act of 21 July 1994 to include the home address of the lessor in the contract lease. Court of Limoges, 28 January 1998.

1998. Residential lease for less than 3 years, article 11 of the Act of 6 July 1989 authorizes the conclusion of a lease for a period of less than 3 years (but at least 1 year) when a specific event that justifies the owner has to return to local reasons professional or family. But two months before term of the contract, the lessor must not forget to confirm the realization of the event. In a case where the owners had not confirmed two months before term lease for a term of two years of their desire return to house their daughter, the Court of Appeal of Versailles that "the lease was automatically extended his term being carried forward automatically to 31 December 1994 (instead of 31 December 1993 originally set). Court of Appeal Versailles 1ère chamber B, 15 May 1998.

1998. Referral of the court: the court cannot be prior to the commission has been itself regardless of whether it has already its opinion. Paris Court of Appeal, 6th Chamber C, March 17 1998.

1998. Job relocation late offer relocation occurred more than a year after the expiration of the lease was reported too late and therefore resulted in the renewal acquiescence of the lease. Supreme Court, 3rd Civil Chamber, 1 July 1998.

1998. Need to rent until the date CCDs leave the termination of the lease, which has effect later, does not make the issue of the rent without object. Supreme Court, 3 rd Civil Chamber, 17 November 1998.

1997. References rent not permitted: are not valid references concerning houses larger than the apartment, the subject of proposed renewal of the lease. Magistrates Court Paris, 27 February 1997. 1997. Accuracy of mixed housing referred: the references did not specify the mixed or non-housing are not accepted. Court, Paris, 13 February 1997. 1997. The notification of the decree of limitation rents in the Paris region in the act of proposed renewal of the lease: No provision of the Act requires the owner to reference to the decree limiting rents in region Paris. Thus, we cannot validly criticize the owner for not having justified the amount of tenant rent renewed under that decree. Court for instance, Paris, 6 February 1997.

1997. The illegal nature of the clause requiring a provider to the lessee, is deemed unwritten clause by which the tenant must sign a contract maintenance of the boiler with a professional imposed by the owner, this does not however the obligation of the tenant to sign a contract maintenance from a professional of his choice. Court for instance, Paris, 4 March 1997.

1997. Form of rent review by the index of cost of construction clause rent review by the index is not automatically subject to any expression of will the owner. Court, Nancy, 18 September 1997.

1997. Exclusion of the ascendant of the spouse of Ownership: the ascendancy of the spouse of an owner does not included in the list of potential benefit from the upturn to live the meaning of Article 15 the Law of 6 July 1989, it is therefore right that the tenant raised the invalidity of leave notified by the lessor to accommodate her stepmother in the housing. Court a forum for Metz, 20 May 1997.

1997. One case of premises: the premises leased by a union in order to accommodate the guardian of a condominium character housing function. Court, Paris, 18 December 1997.

1997. Bail granted by a joint possessor the lease of one well made by one of joint possessors is not zero, it is only effective against other joint possessors and its effectiveness is related to the sort of sharing. Supreme Court, 3rd Civil Chamber, 14 May 1997.

1997. Evidence of the existence of a lease record (occupation of premises by the tenant): judges are sovereign to assess all evidence which they submitted, the only occupation of the premises is not sufficient proof of the quality of the tenant is required: exchanges of correspondence, payment of rent including the existence of receipts to establish proof of initial verbal lease. Supreme Court, 3rd Civil Chamber, 29 April 1997.

1997. Address of owner upon transfer property's holding that there is no changing the meaning of last paragraph of Article 15 of the Act when, following the death usufructuary lessor, the heirs recover the full ownership of the property. Court of Rennes, 18 September 1997.

1996. Wording of the rent: none regulations require the owner to enter on the rent his name and address, particulars necessarily result in the lease. Court of Appeal de Paris, 2 September 1996.

1996. Review of lease record: the annual review of rent by the cost of construction is possible if it is provided in a clause of the lease, the rent of a rented orally, without writing may in fact be revised. Ministerial response, the official newspaper of the National Assembly, 12 August 1996.

1996. The validity of the lease record: the Act of 6 July 1989 requires that the contract be written. In practice, sometimes the lease is oral, the owner and the tenant did not found it useful to materialize the lease by a written document. "The verbal contract executed or under execution is not any; the only opportunity offered to the tenant is request the establishment of a written contract to comply requirements of law ". Court of Appeal of Bourges, 1st Chamber, 29 August 1996.

1995. Remedial rent increases due the ICC (the cost of construction): the Court thinks that not having called time useful increase in rent does not mean waive its profit. The owner can ask his tenant to make up the increase over the last five years. Court of Appeal de Paris, 25 January 1995.

1995. Taking effect of deferred lease and retraction lessee: the lease was signed on 25 February 1992 because some disorders have emerged in the housing tenants do not owe that considered a sum of 135 Euros, corresponding to the conservation, for themselves, the keys to the apartment between 15 and 29 February, the court of first instance sentenced the owner to return the sum to the tenants of 730 EUR retaining that "they had been validly unilaterally terminate the contract, since the discontinuance was served on the owner prior to the date of effective date of the lease. " The Supreme Court considers "In so ruling, while the parties were required the contract from the date of signing and not could be overcome, beyond convention, the conditions provided by law, the court has violated the above texts (Articles 1134 and 1185 of the Civil Code and Article 3 of the Act of 6 July 1989). Supreme Court, 3rd Civil Chamber, Case 19 July 1995.

1995. Rent a storage Chamber: the location of storage is subject to the provisions of the Civil Code, not to those of Law of 6 July 1989. Court, Paris, 10 November 1995.

1995. The removal of rent on wages: Section 4 - d of the Act prohibits a fortiori the clause authorizing the owner to recover the arrears through garnishment. Court, Rennes, December 14 1995.

1995. The partial reference late more consistent, accepted the court: lack of compliance with the requirements of sections 17-c and 19 of the Act of 6 July 1989 as a technicality, if notified two references do not satisfy the requirements, the owner may, during the proceedings, repair the defect by producing more leases compliant. Supreme Court, 3rd Civil Case 1st March 1995.

1995. The difficulty of setting a rent based on References rent: Judge finds that several years use cards provided by the Center rent highlighted the inability to fix in a way reliable rent by reference to rents usually recorded in the area for housing comparable. Court, Paris, 10 October 1995. 1995. The condition clearly undervalued rent ultimately at the discretion of the judge: the undervalued manifesto of rent is a prerequisite for any proposal for revaluation of the lease comes to an term (3 year lease or 6 years in general), the judges background like this sovereign status. Supreme Court, 3rd Civil Chamber, decision of 8 June 1995.

1995. The application of the decree of limitation rents: the effects of a decree issued under Article 18 cover a period at least equal to the length of leases, even though the decree is that all renewable year. Supreme Court, 3rd Civil Case 11 May 1995.

1995. Non-indexation of the rent of the lease record: the Articles 3 and 17 of the Act of 6 July 1989 stipulate that the lessor cannot rely on the rent increase in current lack of indexation clause in fact; no revision rent is possible because a clause expressly mentioned in the lease, and this obviously implies that it is written. Supreme Court, 3rd Civil Chamber, 4 October 1995.

1995. Income of the tenant at the exit of the lease eight years, if tenants are jointly committed to the lessor, we add their resources while As one of them left the scene, since it has not given leave. Supreme Court, 3rd Civil Chamber, 30 May 1995.

1995. References rent and method of financing the property when rents products concern housing subject to the Act of 6 July 1989, tenants cannot oppose the fact that their building has benefited

Even on the initiative of the lessor. Supreme Court, 3rd Civil Case 18 May 1994.

1994. It is the tenant to provide proof of irregularity of the proposal to increase the rent: it is the licensee who has received notification of proposed new rent does not reproduce the Article 17-c to specify and prove the claim that is causing the irregularity. Supreme Court, 3rd Civil Case 9 March 1994.

1994. Lease in time reduced the lessor has applied for the benefit of tenants a lease for a term reduced to two years, indicating he had moved to Paris at the end of this period for reasons professional or family, the Court of Appeal considered that they were deprived of their right of tenure the apartment at the expiration of such period. The Court Supreme stop considering this case that " admit the legality of the lease, the ruling holds that the act The need for one of the owners moved to Paris in the period of two years for business or family, which was a event under the law then the contract specify either the event or the reason for the need to recovery invoked. Supreme Court, 3rd Chamber Civil Case 14 December 1994.

1994. Individual assessment of the age of tenant (Article III-15 of the Act of 6 July 1989): that is the date expiry of the lease that needs to be placed to assess the age the tenant, where there are several tenants for the same lease (egg, husband-tenants) must be consider it sufficient that one of the tenants has exceeded the age of 70 years for all are protected. Supreme Court, 3rd Civil Chamber, 15 June 1994.

1994. Individual income of the tenant (Article III-15 of the Act of 6 July 1989): Just as age customers, the resources of each tenant must be assessed separately. It is therefore not possible to combine the resources of Chamber mates. Supreme Court, 3rd Civil Chamber, 15 June 1994.

1994. Lease to the lessee corporation fault Entry in the scheme of the Act of July 6 1989, the leases entered into by tenants legal persons are normally regime Civil Code. But the parties are free to submit voluntarily their lease with the law of 1989, just as Convention says. Supreme Court, 3rd Chamber Civil Case 12 January 1994.

1994. Application of the cost of construction for an increased rent sixth or third revision of rent by the index, annually on the anniversary of the lease is not inconsistent with the rent increase for sixth, in Consequently, the annual index is combined with increase the annual rent including the first year of the new lease. Supreme Court, 3rd Chamber Civil Case 30 November 1994.

1993. The judges appreciate the sovereign validity of references: for example, judges are not required to seek the arithmetic mean of references, or rely solely on the references annexed to the proposal of the lessor. Supreme Court, 3rd Civil Case 16 November 1993.

1993. Transmission of the lease: a lease mixed-use Housing and professional is transmitted, upon the death of tenant, not to the Crown under section 1742 of Civil Code, but the surviving spouse (who does the heir in the local profession and not living there). Supreme Court, 3rd Civil Chamber, decision of 24 November 1993.

1993. Suspension of the termination clause: the interim order which suspended the effects of termination clause only for the payment of the causes of command and tenants who paid their debt under the conditions prescribed, their deportation a manifestly illegal to do stop. Supreme Court, 3rd Civil Case 16 June 1993.

1993. Renting a garage in the absence of any another lease on a residential dwelling whose location of the garage would have been the enhancement, this location does fall under any regulations. Court
instance Versailles, 9 July 1993.

1993. The remuneration of persons with established the act of lease: notaries, real estate intermediaries, Lawyers involved in the establishment of the act, their remuneration is essential to put the load, half of each party under section 5 of the Act of 6 July 1989. Supreme Court, 3rd Civil Case 19 May 1993.

1993. The parties may agree to an agreement to any time of the procedure: the obligation made parties to the court in the absence of agreement departmental Conciliation Committee does not obstacle to an agreement between the parties. Supreme Court, 3rd Civil Chamber, decision of 23 June 1993.

1993. The garage became attached accessory later in the lease: section 2 does not the need for a single lease and does not rented a garage after the lease in main with the same donor can be considered as principal accessory Housing Tribunal instance Versailles, 9 July 1993.

1993. The property investment company and the duration of lease some SCI are similar to those physical and can therefore enter into leases of three years (Article 10 of the Act of 6 July 1989) and are of the SCI Family and ownerships, and the SCI are those families formed between parents and allies to the fourth degree included.

The owner to prove that it meets the requirements of the law. Court of Appeal of Paris, 6 the Chamber, 15 November 1993.

1993. The possibility of different durations for lease of the garage and the local housing: unless provisions of the two contracting parties aligning the duration of the lease of the premises on the accessory Senior housing, when the two leases were signed in different dates, these leases are independent of terms of duration and the end of the lease does not fact that the premises is incidental to it. Court instance Versailles, 9 July 1993.

1993. Period granted to the tenant after termination of Contract: the termination clause is acquired automatically the tenant is occupying the premises without a title previously leased. The owner is well founded demanding the release of the site, but the judge finds that the acquisition of termination may give the tenant time to organize their departure. Court Montbéliarde instance, 7 July 1993.

1993. Late referral to the court if the surrender of assignment to the secretariat-graft court proceedings occurs after the expiration of the lease contract lease is extended to the previous rent. Supreme Court, 3rd Civil Chamber, decision of 23 June 1993.

1993. Effective date for convenience between Contracting Parties: No provision of the Act of 6 July 1989 prohibits the parties to set a date of effect of the lease other than the signing of the act. Supreme Court, 3rd Civil Chamber, decision of 27 January 1993.

1993. Effective date of lease verbal regularized the lease regularized take effect from the date of the lease but the original record tenant and the owner may agree that the lease has no retroactive effect, as does the lease rewrites begin to run until the adjustment. Supreme Court, 3rd Civil Chamber, 27 January 1993.

1993. Housing concept of function: Government Housing functions are excluded from the scope of the law, which are those "assigned or leased as a result of the exercise of a function or occupation of employment "(Article 2, paragraph 2 the Law of 6 July 1989). Is not considered housing, that subject to a lease entered voluntarily by the employee on the simple means of the employer and whose continuity is independent of the termination of employment contract and therefore, the contract remains subject to the Act of 6 July 1989. Supreme Court, 3rd Civil Chamber, 23 June 1993.

1992. Failure by the tenant in conciliation commission: that the Committee Conciliation duly seized, that it could not make a notice of appearance fault of the tenant does not deprive the lessor's right to go to court. Supreme Court, 3rd Civil Chamber, 15 April 1992.

1992. Proof of the provision of references rent is the owner to prove that he has appended the rent reference to the notification of renewal of lease with a rent increase. Court of Appeal Versailles, 22 May 1992.

1992. The concept of work to improve the equivalent of one year's rent in other examples) have declared inadmissible against the bills tenant by the owner-institutional (work painting for nearly 6 860 Euros on a lock for 381 Euros, the security of the electric installation 1 525 Euros and the rehabilitation of the prosecution for 915 Euros). The Court of Appeal there is work under routine maintenance, major repairs, or contributing maintaining the existing safety and cannot by Therefore, raising of work to improve these latter providing new equipment, service or higher quality level of existing benefits or providing quality to decrease in a manner some expenditure on maintenance or operation or providing greater security of property for people. «Court of Appeal of Paris, 6 the Chamber C, Case 29 January 1992.

1992. Proposal to renew the lease, reproducing the provisions of Article 17-c: Article 17-c of the Act of 6 July 1989 provides that notification of the lessor shall reproduce in full, void, the provisions of Article 17 C of the Act of 6 July 1989. Some argue that this is a nullity absolute, public order, which plays automatically. Stopping the Paris Court of Appeal recalled that "the invalidity of the lessor's proposal for a formal defect consisting non-compliance with the reproduction of the Article 17-c shall not be imposed, pursuant to Article 114 the new Code of Civil Procedure, if this failure caused a complaint to the tenant. " Court of Appeal Paris, 6 the Chamber, 21 May 1992.

1992. Descriptive criteria references rent: Article 5 of the Decree of 31 August 1990 does not need to indicate the date of construction of the building cited references. Court of Appeal of Versailles, 3 April 1992.

1992. Scope of the concept of abandonment of domicile: «departure must be sudden and unpredictable. Thus, when tenant leaves the scene of an agreement with the people living with him, the continuation of the contract has not place ". Court of Appeal of Paris, 6 the Chamber, 29 January 1992.

1992. Bail out of the Act of 1 September 1948 income of the tenant to take into account: for the application of Article 28 of the Act of 23 December 1986 (lease out of eight years) an assessment of income threshold must take account of all income received during the year preceding that in which was formulated proposed contract, whatever their nature, provided they are taxable. It should adopt the same calculation method as the tax administration, after deduction of allowances of 10 and 20%. Supreme Court, 3rd Civil Chamber, decision of 16 December 1992.

1992. The denial of exit from the 1948 Act to lack of income if the tenant intends to rely inadmissibility of the application because the amount of its resources, it must do so within the period of two months, failing which he will be barred. Supreme Court, 3 the Civil Chamber, 17 July 1992.

1992. Rent clearly undervalued another definition : Rent clearly is under-appreciated function of the lowest rents in the neighborhood. Court of Appeal Pau, 19 June 1992.

1992. Duration of the lease by civil society Real estate: the lease term is 3 years old when he comes a civil society family property in the sense of Article 13 - a the Law of 6 July 1989. Supreme Court, 3rd Chamber civil, 25 November 1992.

1991. The effects of the decree limiting rent in the Paris region, "neither the law nor the decree of 27 August 1990 may limit the duration of the effects of this last one year but the validity of the decree itself, so that consequences of the decree during the time it is applicable shall be final.»Magistrates Court, Paris, 5 February 1991.

1991. Concept of geographical area on References rent: the geographical area may be defined by elements such as implantation in the same neighborhood characterized by a certain community architectural, urban, social and commercial. But concept of area remains subject to the discretion Sovereign of the judge. Supreme Court, 3 e Chamber civil, 18 December 1991.

1991. Housing be hired by a legal person is excluded from legislation in June 1982 to December 1986 and July 1989: "subject to the application of Article 57-A, Corporations can benefit from the provisions of the Law of 23 December 1986, nor in the past, the Law of 22 June 1982 and now the law of 6 July 1989; accommodations that are made are subject only to law of the Civil Code. »Supreme Court, 3rd Civil Case 1st June 1991.

1990. Refusal to renew the lease for cause late payment of rent: delays made to the payment of rent are due, in given the absence of some financial difficulties from the tenant, a serious and legitimate reason for refusing to renewal of the lease. Supreme Court, 3 rd Chamber Civil Case April 25 1990.

1990. Amount of work to improve the owner under the decree of limitation Rent: for the owner, the work improvement to take into account when renewing lease, is the share at its expense, which shall be greater than the last year of rent. Court, Paris, 5 April 1990.

1990. The owner can produce references housing that it owns it does not matter whether references supplied by the owner from its own heritage, since these references leases relate freely accepted by the licensees and not subject of litigation challenging the rent of lease. Court, Paris, 1 October 1990.

1990. The distribution of references of rent: in implementation of the Decree of 15 February 1989 (two thirds of References should relate to the present tenants least three years in residence), the court found that should be placed at the effective date of the new lease and use as comparables leases concluded within three years preceding that date. Court, Paris, 9 January 1990.

1990. Continuity of the lease and the right to limit preemption: the Paris Court of Appeal confirmed that the pre-emptive right of the tenant was not applicable when renting the title was not at issue. The lease continues normally with the new owner. Court of Appeal de Paris, 21 February 1990.

1990. Clause illicit site visit: a clause lease requiring the tenant to let go, leave immediately given or received or in case of sale of the building, the leased premises from 9 am to 17 pm on weekdays and from 11 am to 13 pm on Sundays and public holidays, is manifestly excessive and contrary to law because of this Judge limited the right of access 15 hours 17 hours each day. Court, Paris, June 7 1990.

1990. Lease mixed-use and non-compliance with the desegregation usage: the Supreme Court said that non-compliance Joint of the destination of a lease should result in termination. It is, in the case of a lease for residential purposes, with the opportunity for the tenant to exercise its profession as part of the leased premises. The tenant

However, this apartment used for purposes entirely professional setting in the city's offices the company he founded. In so doing, the Court believes that the non-compliance of the destination is a mixed serious breach of the obligations of the location, thus justifying the judicial termination of it. Supreme Court, 3rd Civil Chamber, decision of 30 May 1990.

1990. Sovereign references by the judge: the judge retained the sovereign references Monitor rent. Court, Paris, May 9 1990.

1990. Primacy of the termination clause: the clause resolutory is right for the parties and the judge who is given the respect, since the materiality of the offense is proven. He cannot refuse to apply taking into account the secondary nature of the obligation sanctioned. Supreme Court, 3rd Civil Chamber, 10 May 1990. 1989. Predominance of the last lease explicitly re: a lease originally made under section 3 sexies of the Act of 1 September 1948 was extended by a new lease signed free after expiry.

An appellate court applied by the Supreme Court, considers that by signing a new lease the lessee had abandoned to invoke the law of 1 September 1948 and that the Act was no longer applicable. Supreme Court, 3rd Chamber Civil Case 20 December 1989. 1989. The proposed renewal of the lease originally sent to the tenant outweighs the leave "the lessor who sent the tenant with a proposed renewal of the lease is no longer the possibility to leave. »Magistrates Court, Paris, November 8 1989.

1988. Solicitation of expert opinion by the court: a expert may be appointed with the task of convening, hear the parties and see all the knowledge - INSEE Monitor rent - to provide it with all elements on rents usually found in the neighborhood and comparable homes. Court instance Puteaux, 30 June 1988.

1983. Decommissioning challenge of housing under the 1948 Act the tenant may challenge the decommissioning of its housing by establishing the local does not meet the requirements of Annex I of the Decree of 10 December 1948. Supreme Court, 3rd Civil Chamber, Case 1 June 1983.

CHAPTER VI

VARIOUS SITUATIONS

This involves decisions on matters that may subject to both multiple themes of the Act of July 6 1989; along their sometimes strange or unusual allow are isolated in this chapter.

Examples of case law

2000. Who should pay for the locksmith and remover in case of expulsion? The assistance of a moving company and for a locksmith qualified as a disbursement in the pricing of acts bailiffs (Article 20-3 of Decree No. 96-1080 of 12 December 1996) is correct that an appellate court has found that these costs are the costs. It follows that they may be charged to the party. Supreme Court, 3rd Civil Chamber, decision of 2 March 2000.

2000. The main residence is a concept as administrative and material: the place where the tenant payroll taxes, where he is registered on the lists elections and where it is domiciled; the tenant's family is installed, there is most often and has its main interests. Court of Appeal of Orleans, 31 January 2000.

2000. The tenant cannot object to the installation a dish: the connection of an antenna collective to a wired network, proposed by the lessor, applies to any tenant, since the majority of Tenant has accepted. Supreme Court, 3rd Chamber Civil Case 28 June 2000.

1998. Concept of location as the free or expensive occupation of a dwelling by a third party is not the only criterion for distinguishing the sub-location of simple loan. The Court of Appeal of Grenoble has held that use even free premises by other than tenant, was a sub-lease if it is a prohibited certain duration. In this case, the occupant, a student had two years of study to continue, which implied some permanent and not an occupation it is certain or passing over the tenant's title, unrelated relationship with the occupier, resident elsewhere. Court of Appeal Grenoble, 2nd Chamber, 10 March 998.

1998. Prohibition to take advantage of panel advertising without consent of the owner: the fact to oppose a billboard and receive a payment for the enjoyment of the wall is a sub-lease. The tenant must submit a proposal to the owner. It may therefore oppose the installation. Court of Appeal of Paris, 6th Chamber B, 29 October 1998.

1998. Accident and assessment of an event of force major force majeure shall in the end against the circumstances and attitude of the tenant in the prevention a fire. Supreme Court, 3rd Civil Chamber, Case 18 March 1998.

1998. Establishment of the responsibility of the tenant: the tenant is not exempt from liability if it is established he turned the heating system at the source of a fire without informing the owner. Supreme Court, 3rd Civil Chamber, decision of 10 June 1998.

1998. The tenant has the right to try to install a dish: the lease clause that prohibits tenants to install an antenna is deemed unwritten. Court of Appeal of Paris, 8th Chamber B, 5 February 1998.

1998. The right to an antenna connection: this right is extended to all the TV antennas, regardless of their nature, therefore, are also concerned satellite dishes. Court of Appeal de Paris, 23 the Chamber, 18 November 1998.

1997. Violation of domicile of the lessee by the owner: the owner who has kept a set of key rented housing may be tempted to use them for enter premises without the tenant. The lessor acting and, even in good faith, shall be conviction for home invasion. A tenant had given leave to his owner for a certain date; it has not left the premises on the scheduled date, the owner had taken the initiative to carry its effects in a neighboring apartment was empty, to allow moving new tenants. While recognizing that the mobile-institutional lessor was not foul, the Court of Appeal of Paris has convicted home invasion and damages, Tenant's business had been damaged. Court of Appeal de Paris, 11 e Chamber, 9 September 1997.

1997. Late delivery of keys and payment compensation of occupancy: the tenant, even though had physically left the premises, was sentenced to pay compensation to the owner occupancy (an amount equivalent to the rent due until the actual key) to fault him for not having returned keys. Court of Appeal of Paris, 6th Chamber, B, 9 October 1997 and Supreme Court, 3rd Civil Case 13 November 1997.

1997. Refusal to pay rent: refuse to pay rent, even if the owner does not its own obligations, is illegal. Jurisprudence penalties that attitude, even in If the tenant would rent to a bailiff. Supreme Court, 3rd Civil Chamber, decision of 5 March 1997.

1997. Failure of the tenant insurance: a clause resolutory may relate to the failure of the tenant insurance, the clause is activated; a month after the command sent by the lessor and remained unanswered. Furthermore, in If no such clause, the owner can still take the Judge invoking Article 1184 of the Civil Code. Court of Appeal Paris, 6th Chamber C, 20 May 1997.

1997. The responsibility of the administrator of goods in case of default of the tenant insurance: the administrator's obligation to properly verify that the tenant has purchased insurance. Otherwise, its responsibility may be engaged. Supreme Court, 1st Civil Chamber, decision of 13 May 1997.

1997. The return of the keys to the guard: the return Key was considered validly made in the hands of custodian of the building, even though it had not been appointed for this purpose by the owner, because the eyes tenants, it could appear as mandated by the Owner: "the fact that the same guard himself handed the keys to tenants spouses upon entering places, they could legitimately be considered as the agent of the owner for the receipt of Key to their departure. » Court of Appeal de Paris, 11 the Chamber B, 20 November 1997.

1997. The good faith of the tenant: the termination clause the judge, he cannot suspend or reject its effects to apply whichever considerations related to equity and good faith of the lessee. Supreme Court, 3 rd Civil Division, 5 February 1997.

1997. Clause resolutory abuse: a termination clause does cannot be implemented for non-payment the costs of recovery. Court of Appeal of Paris, 1st July 1997.

1996. Qualification of arson: the fire is often called force majeure, if no evidence has been establishing the responsibility of the tenant, we must not all assume that the tenant is automatically exempt from liability in case of arson. Supreme Court, 3 rd Civil Chamber, 2 October 1996.

1996. Reproduction of law: under Article 24, paragraph 5 "command to pay again, just invalid, the provisions of the preceding paragraphs as well as paragraph 1 of Article 6 of the Act of 31 May

1990 for the implementation of housing rights and giving the option for the tenant to enter the solidarity fund for housing. The inclusion of legal text in the body the bailiff's act is not necessary. Court of Appeal Paris, 6th Chamber B, 28 November 1996. 1996. The maximum interference of the tenant: the tenant does may require to know and verify the content commitments made by the company responsible for the condominium maintenance of common areas of the building, it may require to consult the contract between society and condominiums. Court of Appeal de Paris, 27 September 1996.

1995. Compensation of third parties during the tacit renewal of the lease when the lease been completed shall be extended automatically as Article 1 of the Act of 6 July 1989; the agency, which manages location of the property, cannot ask compensation under Article 5. However, when the lease is renewed explicitly (under Article 17-c) the agency rewrote the contract may request a remuneration to be shared equally between the tenant and the owner as permitted by that Article 5. Answer Ministerial No. 16952, Official Journal of the Assembly National, 5 September 1995.

1995. Home spouse: occupation of a joint dwelling by the tenant and her partner is not a sub-lease and the lessor may refuse consent. No response Ministerial 9158, Official Journal of the National Assembly, 26 January 1995.

1994. Accommodation extended by one third after departure of the holder of the lease: accommodation extended for several years one third of the lease, while the tenant is no longer personally, as the scene is equivalent to an assignment of lease or a sublease, law prohibits both. Court instituting betting, 18 March 1994.

1994. Notification of command: the owner wants to play the termination clause must notify the tenant act by a bailiff. Articles 7 g and 24, paragraph 1 of Law 6 July 1989 require the issuance of a command by bailiff or by registered letter receipt. Supreme Court, 3rd Civil Chamber, 31 May 1994.

1993. Clarification on Article 5: If the lessor, person physical or moral ensures its own all approaches, it is not entitled to any remuneration for this service. Answer Ministerial No. 66511, Official Journal of the Assembly National, 29 March 1993.

1993. Concept of free rent in a lease may be concluded for a nominal fee but it cannot be accepted for derisory price, equivalent to no bail. Supreme Court, 3rd Civil Chamber, decision of 27 October 1993.

1993. Location of the garage alone: if housing is be leased to a person and a garage located or not in the same residence, for another completely separate person, the rental of the garage will be governed by common law and not by the law of 6 July 1989. Likewise, rental of the garage will only law. Supreme Court, 3rd Civil Chamber, 23 June 1993.

1992. A duty to issue a receipt to lessee when a owner fails to issue receipts to the tenant, equivalent to payment terms, thus depriving him of the possibility of recover rent as it is considered being in bad faith and cannot invoke the clause resolutory under lease. Supreme Court, 3rd Chamber Civil Case 17 June 1992.

1992. Area of the termination clause: Article 4 of the g Law of 6 July 1989 provides four possible cases clause resolutory, which are the defaults rents, charges, deposit and non-subscription of a rental insurance risk. The clauses for another reason are considered "non-written" by the law and therefore declared inadmissible. Court of Appeal Paris, 6th Chamber C, 25 February 1992.

1991. The case of nonpayment of rent amount does not stop the reality of the contract: the contract location may provide a payment out species, egg against the payment of repairs, but the Convention would have to be different loan at no charge. Supreme Court, 3 rd Civil Chamber, decision of 4 January 1991.

1991. Difference between accommodation and subleasing the tenant is free to receive and accommodate any person if it is temporary. From when he installs in his apartment or in an independent part of it a person who is not a member of his family and for a long time, it must obtain the consent of its owner. Court, Paris, 19 June 1991.

1990. Payments of an occupant without title does not qualify for lease has been broken the court's decision of Appeal of Paris which concluded that the owner has accepted are paid by an occupant without title, implicitly accepts the existence of a rental bond. Indeed, it there can be no presumption of bail when the owner accepts payments in exchange for an occupation a local, even if the author would have paid qualified them to rent. Supreme Court, 3rd Chamber Civil Case 7 June 1990.

1989. Possession of pets: In principle, possession of pets a tenant is permitted to the extent that the presence of these animals adds no trouble to the neighbors and this is confirmed the Supreme Court, rejecting a ruling from the court of appeal, which did not establish whether the presence of many animals did not odors to neighbors.

Supreme Court, 3 rd Civil Chamber, decision of 28 June 1989. 1989. Housing Concierge Service: Housing function is excluded from the scope of the Act of 6 July 1989 but is still governed by the Civil Code. The judge refuses to expel the concierge when his employer did notified leave a month after the cessation of job. Court of Appeal of Versailles, 13 September 1989.

CHAPTER VII

LITIGATION AND NEGOTIATION LEGAL ROCEEDINGS

1. Letter with acknowledgment of receipt (letter AR) or notification by a bailiff. When renewing the lease, after six or three years, the owner shall notify its proposed increase in rent, either by registered letter with acknowledgment of receipt, or by Usher. Procedure:
- A) the notification must be received by the tenant 6 months before the expiry of the lease;
- B) the tenant gives his answer 4 months before the same deadline
- c) the lessee does not respond, the owner must interpret this silence as a refusal, it can - and the tenant for that matter - take the department conciliation;
- D) failing agreement by the Committee conciliation, the owner must enter the court of the place where the housing and when does not before the expiry of the lease it is tacitly. For the owner, the choice of the bailiff is a guarantee that the proposal comes to the tenant because without this last or when the tenant refuses to move look for the letter is usually expense of the owner that the judges decide. For the tenant, including the oldest, the act bailiff, permitted by the Act of 6 July 1989, must be appreciated as a normal procedure, should not be panic or be scandalized, it should be possibly negotiate with the owner or manager housing or to prepare the discussion in committee departmental conciliation.
2. The free negotiation or commission departmental conciliation it should be remembered that the Act of 6 July 1989 aims to govern "the reports rental" and it would be a shame to overlook this step and directly join in logic of conflict. The tenant has an interest in

about rent levels in its neighborhood, to open to negotiation when possible.

In this negotiation, beyond the numbers reported, we may also mention the state of housing, the failure any services, pollution, etc... In departmental Conciliation Committee: it is composed of representatives of tenants and owners. For minutes of the meeting, she his view, so both sides will get finally that what each Please give at conciliation; it will incorporate the possibility of making concessions; the presence of a lawyer is not mandatory but can be assisted by any person of his choice.

3. The magistrates Court

when the bilateral negotiations and the transition to the Committee did not reach an agreement, the owner must take all measures to enter the court of the whereabouts of the dwelling; there is a canton or arrondissement of Paris. The court before the mandatory date expiry of the lease, so the referral must also be placed at the court in the same delay.

Form of application: the referral to the court by letter with acknowledgment receipt, addressed to the Registry by a party. The procedure for passage before the court - A) Prepare and issue the summons with the help of a legal professional, the assignment shows the days and hours the audience: it issued 15 days before the hearing; the delivery of the summons must intervene at the court at least 8 days before the hearing date.

- B) Place the subpoena in court.

- C) To audience (there may be several passages in audience), the court shall summon the parties hearing by letter charged with receiving, also warning the defendant that if appearance, it is exposed to what the decision is made against him solely on the evidence provided by the applicant.

- D) Share the findings and the parties in presence should provide all the evidence they pay to the file; everything that is sent to the court must be brought to the attention of the opposing party.

- E) Make a file argument, in the light of the argument, the judge indicates the date on which the trial should be made, as the case is ready for trial or not, he may order one or more references, including direct the parties to go before the Committee departmental conciliation where the date Session adopted the latter is later than the court or simply, if we failed to grasp the Committee.

- F) Finally, the judge pronounced the verdict, in fact, the judge seek to reconcile the two parties, but failing to get the case is tried. The trial involved in general 1 or 2 months after hearing oral argument.

4. The interim ruling of the court

The procedure: The procedure is frequently referred used in real estate, for example appoint an expert, get the eviction of a tenant after trigger a termination clause, grant deadlines payment to the debtor, to obtain supplies on sums due or request a deposit of rents in anticipation of work to be done by the owner. Advantage: the procedure for relief is faster than usual procedure. Indeed, the judge decides   in all cases of emergency, if there is no serious challenge. The procedure for the assignment: the assignment is given by Usher, usually 10 days before the hearing and placed at the court. After the passage, hearing is made, the trial involved 15 days after if the defender does not serious, in which case, the court shall declare incompetent, forcing the plaintiff to pursue ordinary. 5. To appeal the ruling of the court it is mandatory to be represented by a lawyer who advocate. The deadline for appeals court forum is one month for regular judgments and 15 days for those delivered in relief. The significance of assignment is being done by a bailiff is the starting point of this period. Overall, the appeal process can take 1 to 2 years.

6. The cost of the move to court

Costs: they are the responsibility of those who lost trial, but other costs, particularly fees attorneys are at the discretion of the judge who has a large power of decision, the costs are those costs expertise and bailiff's fees. In the court of first instance bailiff's fees are reflected mainly the cost of acts of a bailiff. Thus, the party loses the case is principle to bear the costs.
Compensation for the winning party the judge may be requested to order the losing party to pay another costs other than expense, such as attorneys' fees; the judge takes into account the economic situation of the sentenced, with an equity research. The judge may wholly or partially grant or deny - the cost incurred by the opposing party - the winner, knowing that Here, he has great freedom of

choice.

Attorneys' fees: the fees are free and subject to the scale of the Bar Association. Typically, billing is done - at least in part - as a function of time that counsel spent on the case, but time is also a variable depending on the difficulty and the uncertainties of each case. The billing may take into maxima of packages or be calculated according to the result. However, the individual may request a judicial assistance, on file with the clerk of court his home.

7. Enter the Supreme Court

this is the highest court and is located in Paris. She controls the regularity of law. It examines whether the Court of Appeal properly applied the law. Before that court, the parties are obliged to have recourse to a lawyer for advice. The appeal process is lengthy and expensive and is advised not to engage in this process so that if significant interests are at stake or requirements of principle or to honor defend.

8. Approaches useful in the Paris area

Owners' association and owners
123, rue Saint-Lazare
75008 Paris.
Tel: 01 43 87 56 65

Association official's condominium
27, rue Joseph Python
75020 Paris
Tel: 01 40 30 12 82
Website: www.asso-gsp.org

House owners - National Union of Property real estate (UNPI) -
Paris-Ile-de-France
74, rue de Longchamp
75116 Paris
Tel: 08 92 70 71 15
Website: www.csppc.asso.fr

Tenants Associations General Confederation of housing
14, rue Frédéric Lemaître

75020 Paris
Tel: 01 43 66 49 11

Confédération Nationale du logement - Federation of Paris, all districts
62, boulevard Richard Lenoir
75011 Paris
Tel: 01 47 00 96 20

Independent Federation of Tenants
12, rue des Ashtrays
75020 Paris
Tel: 01 40 33 96 42 77

Legal acts and technical expertise Departmental Chamber of Bailiffs
17, rue de Beaujolais
75001 Paris
Tel: 01 42 96 19 46

Chambre des notaires
1, boulevard Sebastopol
75001 Paris
Tel: 01 44 82 24 00

National real estate experts
18, rue Volney
75002 Paris
Tel: 01 42 96 18 46

House of real estate in France
19, rue du Faubourg Saint-Honoré
75008 Paris
Tel: 01 53 76 03 52

Departmental conciliation Paris
50, avenue Daumesnil
75012 Paris
Tel: 01 49 28 40 00

Hauts-de-Seine (prefecture)

167, avenue F & I Joliot Curie
92013 Nanterre cedex
Tel: 01 40 97 20 20 / 08 21 80 30 92
Website: www.hauts de seine.pref.gouv.fr

Seine-Saint-Denis (prefecture)
124, rue Carnot
93000 Bobigny
Tel: 01 41 60 60 60 / 08 21 80 30 93

Val-de-Marne (Préfecture)
Avenue du Général de Gaulle
94000 Créteil
Tel: 01 49 56 60 60
www.val de marne.pref.gouv.fr

Yvelines (Prefecture)
1, rue Jean Houdon
78000 Versailles
Tel: 01 39 49 78 00

Obtain references rent for the Region Parisienne monitor rental
from Paris agglomeration (OLAP)
21, rue Miollis
75015 Paris
Tel: 01 40 56 01 47
Website: www.olap.asso.fr

Manufacturers of standard contracts Note: the leases of the various
publishers are available in bookstores.
Printing Tissot
19, rue Lagrange
75005 Paris
Tel: 01 44 41 71 11

De particulier à particulier
40, rue du Docteur Roux
75015 Paris
Tel: 01 40 56 33 33

Hestia (real estate between individuals), headquartered

80, rue Gallieni
92100 Boulogne-Billancourt
Tel: 01 55 60 56 56

Advice and information multifaceted
Department of Infrastructure, Transport, Housing,
Tourism and the Sea

- Directorate General for Urban Planning and Habitat of the
construction –
Arche de La Défense
92055 Paris la Défense Cedex 04
Tel: 01 40 81 21 22
Website: www.logement.equipement.gouv.fr

Ville de Paris: Information Office of the owners and
occupants (BIPO)
6, rue Agrippa d'Aubigné
75004 Paris
Tel: 01 42 76 31 31

Association departmental information on housing
(ADIL 75 ANIL in Paris and throughout France)
45 bis, boulevard Edgar Quinet
75014 Paris
Tel: 01 42 79 95 50
Website: www.anil.org

Legislation: Official Journal (J O)
26, rue Desaix
75015 Paris
Tel: 01 40 58 75 00
Website: www.journal-officiel.gouv.fr
website (French law): www.legifrance.gouv.fr

CHAPTER VIII

MAIN DECREES APPLICATION
THE LAW OF 6 JULY 1989

A. LIST OF REPAIRS TO THE INCUMBENT TENANT

- Full text –

Decree No. 87-712 of 26 August 1987 under Article 7 of Law No. 86-1290 of 23 December 1986 seeking to encourage investment in rental, home ownership housing and development of land supply for repairs and rental.
NOR: EQUC8700032D
Prime Minister
on the report of the Minister of State, Minister of Economy, Finance and Privatization, the Keeper of the Seals, Minister of Justice and Minister for Infrastructure, housing, Planning and transport Having regard to Law No. 86-1290 of 23 December 1986 to encourage investment in rental, home ownership of housing and development of land supply, particular Article 7 (d);
the Council of State (Section of Public Works) course
Article 1.

Leasehold repairs are maintenance work current and minor repairs, including replacement of elements akin to say repairs resulting from normal use of premises and equipment for private use. Including the nature of the tenant's repairs repairs listed in the annex to this decree.

Article 1 bis (Decree No. 99-667 of 26 July 1999, art. 1, OJ 1 August 1999).
This decree is applicable to French Polynesia the implementation of Article 7 of Law No. 89-462 of 6 July 1989. List of repairs with the repair Leasehold Appendix
I - External Parties which the tenant has exclusive use
a) Private Gardens:
maintenance, including driveways, lawns, massive ponds and pools; size, pruning, weeding tree and shrubs, bushes replacement, repair and replacement of mobile sprinklers.
b) Awnings, canopies and terraces: removal of moss and other plants.
c) down storm water gutters and gutters: crocking ducts.

II - internal and external openings

  a) Sections such as opening doors and windows: lubrication of hinges, hinges and hinges; minor repairs buttons and door handles, the hinges, Cremona replacement including bolts, pins and target.
  b) Glazing:
  c) repair of sealants; replacement of deteriorated windows. devices obscuration of light such as stores and jealousy: lubrication; including replacement of ropes, pulleys or few blades.
  d) Locks and Security Locks:
     lubrication; replacement of small parts and lost keys or damaged.
  e) Grids: cleaning and lubrication.

III - to interior Including replacement of bolts, pins, targets

     a) ceilings, interior walls and partitions:
     maintenance of cleanliness; menus connections paintings and tapestries; restoration or replacement of some elements of coating materials such as ceramics, mosaics, plastics; backfilling holes made similar to compensation by the number, size and the location thereof.
b) Wooden floors, carpets and other floor coverings: and usual glazing; replacement blades for a few floors and refurbishing state, laying carpet fittings and other coatings soil, notably in case of stains

in addition, holes.

c) Placards and woodwork such as skirting boards, rods and trim: Replacement cleats for shelves and cupboards and repair their closing device; setting fittings and replacing spikes joinery.

IV - Plumbing installations

a) Water Pipes:
crocking; including replacement of gaskets and clamps.
b) gas pipeline:
maintenance of valves, siphons and openings ventilation; replacement of hoses connection.
c) Septic tanks, cesspools and cesspits: drain.
d) Heating, hot water and valves:
replacement of bimetal, pistons, diaphragms, boxes water, valves and seals gas appliances; rinsing and cleaning of heating and piping; replacement of gaskets, valves and cable glands for valves; replacement of seals, gaskets and floats bells toilet flushing.
e) Sinks and fixtures:
cleaning limestone deposits, replacement of pipes Flexible shower.

V - Equipment of electricity installations

Replacement of switches, sockets, coupe circuits and fuses, light bulbs, luminous tubes; repair or replacement of ducts or chopsticks protection.

VI - Other equipment mentioned in the lease

a) Routine maintenance and minor repairs of equipment such as refrigerators, washing machines and washer, dryer, range hoods, water softeners, solar collectors, heat pumps, devices air conditioning, individual antennas radio and television, furniture sealed chimneys, lenses and mirrors.
b) Petty repairs necessitated by the removal of flanges.
c) lubrication and replacement of seals drainers.
d) Chimney sweeping of ducts and smoke Gas and ventilation ducts.
Article 2

The Minister of State, Minister of Economy, Finance and privatization, the Keeper of the Seals, Minister of Justice, and Minister of Equipment, Housing, Physical Planning territory and transport are responsible, in their which, for the implementation of this Decree, which will be published in the Official Journal of the French Republic.

By the Prime Minister:

Jacques Chirac

The Minister for Infrastructure, housing,

Planning and transport Pierre Méhaignerie.

The Minister of State, Minister of Economy, Finance and privatization Édouard Balladur.

The Keeper of the Seals, Minister of Justice,

Albin Chalandon.

B. LIST OF CHARGES RECOVERABLE INCUMBENT THE TENANT

- Full text –

Decree No. 87-713 of 26 August 1987 under Article 18 of Law No. 86-1290 of 23 December 1986 to encourage investment rental home - ownership of housing and development land supply and determining the list of recoverable costs. NOR: EQUC8700582D

Prime Minister
on the report of the Minister of State, Minister of Economy, Finance and Privatization, the Keeper of the Seals, Minister of Justice and Minister for Infrastructure, housing, Planning and transport Having regard to Law No. 86-1290 of 23 December 1986 to encourage investment in rental, home ownership of housing and development of land supply and particular Article 18; the Council of State (Section of Public Works) course
Article 1

The list of charges recoverable under Article 18 of the Law of 23 December 1986 referred to above is annexed to this Decree.
Article 2
For the purposes of this Decree:

a) There is no need to distinguish between the services provided by the lessor in governance and services provided under a contract for services. The cost of insured services Governance includes the expenses of management staff technique. Where there is a business contract, the lessor must ensure that the contract distinguishes between expenditure recoverable and other expenses.
b) Personnel costs are recoverable
Remuneration and social charges and tax; c) The maintenance of common parts and the elimination discharges are provided by a guardian or caretaker, the expenditure corresponding to his salary, excluding wages in kind are payable in respect of charges recoverable in respect of three quarters of their amount.
d) The maintenance of common parts and the elimination discharges are provided by an employee of building, expenditure cor-

responding to his salary and expenses social and tax thereon shall be payable in full, in as charges recoverable. The replacement of equipment is considered as akin to small repairs if the cost is equal to the cost thereof.

Article 3

For the purposes of this Decree, the costs to routine maintenance and minor repairs individual facilities, which appear in Table III attached, are recoverable when made by the donor instead of the tenant. Article 3 bis (Decree No. 99-667 of 26 July 1999, s.2, OJ 1 August 1999).
This decree is applicable to French Polynesia implement the provisions of Article 23 of Law No. 89-462 of 6 July 1989.
List of charges recoverable.

Appendix

I - Elevators and lifts

1 Cost of electricity.
2 operating expenses, maintenance, minor repairs.

a) Operations:
- Periodic inspection, cleaning and lubrication of the organs mechanical;
- Biannual review of cables and annual audit of parachutes;
- Annual cleaning of the bowl, the top of the cab and of machinery;
- Troubleshooting not requiring repairs or supplies parts;
- Maintenance of a file by the maintenance company stating technical visits, and significant incidents involving the device.
b) Provision relating to products or small equipment maintenance (rags, greases and oils needed) and lighting of the cabin.
c) Petty repairs:
- The cabin (sending buttons, door hinges, contacts doors, automatic door closers, slides cabin safety device threshold and photocell);
- Bearings (mechanical door closers, electric or tires, electromechanical locks, contacts door and call buttons); brushes of the motor and fuses.

II - Cold water, hot water and space heating Private and

parts in common.

1 Expenditure on:

in cold water and hot tenants or occupants of building or the buildings housing concerned; to water needed for maintenance parts common or those buildings, including the station purification; to water needed for maintenance of space external; expenditure on water consumption include all taxes and fees and the sums due under the charge of sanitation, exclusion those to which the owner is required in application of Article L. 35-5 of the Public Health Code; products necessary for the operation, maintenance and water treatment; to electricity; fuel or energy supply, whatever its nature.

2 operating expenses, maintenance and small repairs :
   a) Operation and maintenance:
      - Cleaning nozzles, electrodes, filters and valves for burners;
      - Maintenance and lubrication pump relay gauges, level controllers nod groups motor pumps sumps and pumps;
      - Lubrication of valves and faucets and repair of presses stoups;
      - Replacement of bulbs and lights bulbs boiler;
      - Maintenance and adjustment of the apparatus of regulation automatic and its annexes;
      - Verification and maintenance of regulators draw;
      - Adjustment of valves, taps and activities do not include balancing;
      - Purge points heating;
      - Cost of combustion controls;
      - Maintenance of smoke scrubbers;
      - Procedure in rest at the end of heating season flushing the heater and pipes, cleaning boiler Chambers, including sumps and drains, chimney boilers, flues and chimneys;
      - Conducting heat;
      - Rental fees for maintenance and meter reading general and individual;

- Maintenance of the water softener, cleaners of water on the and reassure regulator;
- Periodic inspections to prevent leakage of fluid refrigerant heat pumps;
- Checking, cleaning and lubrication of the organs of heat pumps;
- Periodic cleaning of the outside sensors solar;
- Checking, cleaning and lubrication of the organs of solar collectors.

b) Petty repairs in common areas or on items of common use:
- Repair of leaks on fittings and joints;
- Replacement of joints, valves and cable glands;
- Lapping valve seats;
-Minor repairs to address the leakage of fluid refrigerant heat pumps - recharge fluid refrigerant heat pumps.

III - Individual installations

Heating and hot water, water in the private

1 Cost of fuel supply common.

2 Operation and maintenance, minor repairs.

a) Operation and maintenance:
- Adjustment of flow and temperature of the hot water;
- Checking and adjustment of equipment, enslavement, security aqua stat and pump;
- Troubleshooting;
- Check connections and nutrition electric water heaters, controls the intensity absorbed;
- Verification of the status of resistors, thermostats, cleaning;
- Setting thermostats and temperature control water;
- Monitoring and repairing water tightness of connections cold - hot water;
- Control of security groups;
- Lapping valve seats of valves;
- Setting mechanisms for flushing toilets.

b) Petty repairs:

- Replacement of bimetal, pistons, diaphragms, boxes water, - valves and seals gas appliances;
- Rinsing and cleaning of heating and piping;
- Replacement of joints, valves and cable glands for valves;
- Replacement of joints, floaters and attached bells toilet flushing.

IV - Common domestic building or all residential buildings.
1 Expenditure on:

a) electricity

b) For supplies, including products maintenance, brush and small equipment needed to be treated maintenance of cleanliness, salt.

2 Operation and maintenance, minor repairs:

a) Maintenance of the timer, installation, removal and maintenance carpet.
b) Petty repairs appliances maintenance of cleanliness such aspirators. 3 Maintenance of cleanliness (payroll).

V - areas outside the building or the completely residential buildings (roads, parking and surrounding green spaces, areas and play equipment).

1 Expenditure on: to electricity; for petrol and oil; consumable supplies used in the maintenance Current light bulbs or tubes for lighting, fertilizers, bactericide and insecticide products such as seeds, flowers, plants for replacement, excluding those used for repair of massive beds or hedges.
2 Operation and maintenance:

a) The operations of cutting, weeding, weeding, raking, cleaning and watering of:

- Driveways, parking areas and landscaping; green space (lawns, massive, shrubs, hedges, beds);
- Playgrounds;
- Ponds, fountains, gutters, pipes disposal of storm water;
- Maintenance of horticultural equipment;
- Replacement of sand trays and small equipment games.
b) Painting and minor repairs of benches and gardens playground equipment and fences.

VI - Hygiene.

1 Cost of consumables:
plastic bags and paper to remove discharges; products on disinfection and disinfection, including columns dry garbage dump.
2 Operation and maintenance:
Maintenance and emptying of cesspools; maintenance of equipment packaging waste.
3 Elimination of discharges (payroll).

VII - Miscellaneous equipment of the building or the whole houses

1 The provision of energy needed for ventilation mechanics.
2 Operation and maintenance:
chimney ventilation ducts; maintenance of mechanical ventilation; maintenance of automatic or encoded and intercoms; periodic visits with the exception of controls safety regulations, cleaning and lubricating apparatus fixed handling nacelles cleaning glass facades.
3 Others:
Post of subscription phone available for tenants.

VIII - taxes and royalties.

Right to lease.
Tax or fee for garbage collection.
Tax scan.
Article   4
The Minister of State, Minister of Economy, Finance and privatiza-

tion, the Keeper of the Seals, Minister of Justice, and Minister of Equipment, Housing, Physical Planning territory and transport are responsible, in their which, for the implementation of this Decree, which will be published in the Official Journal of the French Republic. By the Prime Minister:

Jacques Chirac.
The Minister for Infrastructure, housing,
Planning and transport Pierre Méhaignerie.
The Minister of State, Minister of Economy, Finance and privatization Édouard Balladur.
The Keeper of the Seals, Minister of Justice,
Albin Chalandon.

C. THE CRITERIA DESCRIPTIONS REFERENCES RENT

- Full text –

Decree 90-781 of 31 August 1990 concerning the application of Articles 30 and 31 of Law No. 86-1290 of 23 December 1986 amended.
NOR: LOGC9000075D

Prime Minister

on the report of the Minister Delegate to the Minister of Infrastructure, Housing, Transport and the Sea for Housing,
Having regard to Law No. 86-1290 of 23 December 1986, as amended, and particular Articles 30 and 31;
Having regard to Decree No. 87-818 of 2 October 1987 establishing the list of common part of an agglomeration of more than 1 000 000 inhabitants;
Having regard to the opinion of the National Consultative Commission dated 23 March 1990

Article   1
To enable the application of Articles 30 and 31 of the Act of 23 December 1986, rents are used as references be representative of all rents usually observed over the past three years in the neighborhood for comparable housing, whatever the date of entry into the premises of the tenant.
The list of references notified by the owner must include the elements set out in Articles 2, 3, 4 and 5 this Decree.

Article 2

The minimum number of references to be provided shall be three. However, it is six in the common part an agglomeration of more than 1 000 000 inhabitants contained in Decree No. 87-818 of 2 October 1987 referred to above.

Article 3

The references must be taken in the vicinity housing in question, either in the same group of buildings or in any other group buildings

with similar characteristics and located in the same geographical area.
Article 4

The list of references notified by the lessor must bear at least two-thirds of the references of locations for which there was no change of tenant past three years.
Article 5

References for determining the rent under Articles 30 and 31 of the Act of 23 December 1986 above include for each of them:
a) the name of the street and the dozen numbers where the building;
b) the quality and timing of construction of the building;
c) the floor of the housing and the possible presence of a lift
d) The floor area of housing and many of its major parts;
e) the existence of schedules taken into account for the rent;
f) the status of equipment: in particular, WC inside, Chamber water heating;
g) an indication that the tenant is in places since more or less than three years;
h) the amount of monthly rent effectively excluding required.
Article 6

Decree No. 89-98 of 15 February 1989 is repealed as it concerns the application of Articles 30 and 31 of the Act of 23 December 1986 referred to above.

Article 7

The Minister of State, Minister of Economy, Finance and budget, the Keeper of the Seals, Minister of Justice, the Minister for Infrastructure, Housing, Transport and the sea, the Minister Delegate to the Minister of Infrastructure, Housing, Transport and the Sea of Housing and Secretary of State, with the Minister of State, Minister of Economy, Finance and budget, for consumption, shall, each in this regard, the implementation of this Decree, which will be published in the Official Journal of the French Republic.
By the Prime Minister:

Michel Rocard.
Minister Delegate to the Minister of Infrastructure,
housing, transport and marine, in charge of housing,
Louis Besson.
The Minister of State, Minister of Economy, Finance and budget
Pierre Bérégovoy.
The Keeper of the Seals, Minister of Justice,
Pierre Méhaignerie.
The Minister for Infrastructure, Housing, Transport and of the sea,
Michel Delebarre.
Secretary of State to the Minister of State, Minister of Economy,
Finance and Budget, responsible for consumption, Veronique
Neiertz.

D. MINIMUM AND COMFORT HABITABLE HOUSING

Decree No. 87-149 of 06 March 1987 laying down the conditions minimum of comfort and livability to be meeting the premises available for rent. NOR: EQUC8700007D

Prime Minister
on the report of the Keeper of the Seals, Minister of Justice, and the Minister for Infrastructure, housing, Planning and transport Having regard to the Public Health Code, including Title I; Having regard to the labor code;
having regard to the Code of Construction and Housing; Having regard to Law No. 48-1360 of 1 September 1948 as mended on modification and codification of legislation on reports of owners and tenants or occupants of premises residential or professional use and establishing housing allowances;
Having regard to Law No. 86-1290 of 23 December 1986 to encourage investment in rental, home ownership of housing and development of land supply and in particular Articles 6, 25, 26, 28, 31 and 35.

Article 1

The standards listed in Article 25 of the Act of 23 December 1986 referred to above are:
1 Housing in residential or part of premises mixed-use residential and professional to housing must have the following characteristics:
a) Composition and dimensions:
A housing includes at least one piece housing and adjoining parts of the service include: kitchen or kitchenette, bathroom and toilets, it may be located in the bath room, this Chamber housing must have at least nine square meters where the kitchen is separated or at least twelve square meters where there is a kitchen. The height of dwellings and the kitchen is not less than two meters twenty. However, it may be less than two meters twenty, without being less than two meters, if the dwelling has not undergone division in height from 1 September 1948.
The surface area is determined in accordance with Article R 111-2 of the Code of Construction and Housing.
b) Opening and breakdown:

Any piece housing has an opening giving outside the building allowing for ventilation and a sufficient illumination and ensuring the proper use of housing and conservation of the building. Every piece is provided with an opening giving outside the building or, alternatively, has a drainage system leading to the exterior of the building and ensuring the efficient use of housing and conservation this building.

  c) Kitchen or kitchenette:

    The kitchen or the kitchen is inside and includes a sink with drain connected to a drop of water on which is installed drinking water cold and hot water. The kitchen or kitchenette is fitted to receive a device for cooking (gas or electric) or has a vent pipe smoke in good condition.

  d) Bathroom and toilets:

    The bathroom is inside the housing, is a separate Chamber and has a bath or shower and a sink with drains and fed hot water and Cold.

    The toilets are inside the housing, are a separate Chamber, unless it is part of the Chamber water and have a bowl in the English and a flush. If fitted with a watertight pit, hunting water may be replaced by simple water. The toilets are separated from the kitchen and the Chamber where meals are eaten.

    The floors are sealed and the walls around the shower and tub are protected against infiltration. e) Gas and electricity:

    Housing is supplied with electricity and, where appropriate, gas. These feeds, and the breakdown of parts where gas is used to meet normal requirements of users, these facilities must ensure the safety of users. New electrical installations and new gas potential, and the breakdown of Chambers where the gas is used, comply with regulation.

  e) Water:

    The domestic water installations provide housing permanence of the distribution with pressure and flow sufficient.

    2. The part of the premises for professional use as well as premises complies with the legislation in force hygiene and safety.

3. Floors, walls, ceilings or local housing above show no infiltration or rising water.

The openings are watertight and in good condition operation.

4. The building does not present a serious lack of maintenance.

The large opening (walls, roofs, stairs, floors, balconies) is in good condition.

Coverage, its fittings and accessories are watertight.

Article 2

The standards listed in Article 1 of this Decree apply to leases entered into pursuant to the second paragraph of Article 3 of the Act of 1 September 1948 above.

Article 3

Except for disputes pending before the courts, the decree No. 78-924 of 22 August 1978 is hereby repealed.

Article 4

The Keeper of the Seals, Minister of Justice and Minister of Infrastructure, Housing, Spatial Planning and Transport is responsible, in their respective fields, the implementation of this Decree, which will be published in the Journal Official of the French Republic.

By the Prime Minister:

Jacques Chirac.

The Minister for Infrastructure, Housing,

Regional Planning and Transport,

Pierre Méhaignerie.

The Keeper of the Seals, Minister of Justice,

Albin Chalandon.

E. CHARACTERISTICS OF DECENT HOUSING

Decree No. 2002-120 of 30 January 2002 on decent housing characteristics for the application of Article 187 of Law No. 2000-1208 of
13 December 2000 on solidarity and urban renewal.

NOR: EQUU0200163D

Prime Minister
on the report of the Minister for Infrastructure, Transport and housing :
Having regard to the civil code;
having regard to the Code of Construction and Housing, including
Articles L 111-1 and L 111-2;
Having regard to Law No 67-561 of 12 July 1967 on improving of
habitat;
Having regard to Law No. 89-462 of 6 July 1989 to improve the
rental reports and amending Act No. 86-1290
23 December 1986, particularly Articles 2 and 6 in Following the
drafting of Article 187 of Law No. 2000-1208 of 13 December
2000 relating to solidarity and urban renewal;
Having regard to Decree No. 68-976 of 9 November 1968 laying
down conditions of application of Law No. 67-561 of 12 July 1967
on improving habitat; After consulting the National Housing dated
10 May 2001;
Having regard to the opinions of the Regional Council of Guadeloupe dated 31 August 2001, the General Council of Guadeloupe
dated 13 September 2001 and the General Council Meeting dated 3
October 2001;
Having regard to the letters of referral for the opinion of the regional Guyana, Martinique Regional Council and the Board Regional Meeting dated August 9, respectively, 10 August and 10 August
2001;
Having regard to the letters of referral for the opinion of the General Council of Guyana and the General Council of Martinique in
date respectively, 9 August and 10 August 2001;
The Council of State (Section of Public Works) course
Article 1

Decent housing is housing that meets the characteristics defined by this decree.
Article 2

Housing must meet the following conditions, the regard to the physical safety and health of tenants:

1) It provides the closed and covered. The bulk of the housing opens and its access is properly maintained and strength and protects against local runoff and rising water. The external joinery and

   coverage with its fittings and accessories provide protection against water penetration into the home. For dwellings located in the overseas departments, it may be taken into account in assessing the conditions Protection against the infiltration of water, climatic conditions specific to these departments.

2) The restraints of the people in the housing and access, such as railings, windows, staircases, loggias and balconies, are in a state consistent with their use.

3) The nature and state of conservation and maintenance construction materials, piping and Housing coatings do not pose risks obvious health and physical safety of tenants.
   4) The networks and connections of electricity and gas and heating and hot water conform to safety standards set by the laws and regulations and are in good condition for use and operation.

4) Devices for opening and ventilation of dwellings allow a renewal of air adapted to the needs normal occupation of a housing and operation equipment.

5) The main parts, the meaning of the third paragraph of Article R 111-1 of the Code of Construction and Housing have sufficient natural lighting and an opening giving the open air or on a volume glass giving the air free.
   Article 3

The accommodation comprises of equipment and comfort following:
1) A facility for a normal heating, fitted devices for power supply and disposal combustion products and suitable to the characteristics of housing. For dwellings located in the

departments overseas, it may not be applied these provisions if weather conditions warrant.

2) A facility for supplying potable water to ensure inside the housing with the pressure distribution and a flow sufficient for normal use of its tenants.

3) Installations of domestic waste water and sewage to prevent the growing of odors and effluent and with siphon.

4) A kitchen or kitchenette equipped to receive a cooking appliance including a sink connected to a supply of hot water and Cold and installation of sewage disposal.

5) A plumbing domestic housing including c, separated from the kitchen and the Chamber where made meals, and equipment for the toilet body, having a bath or shower, furnished to ensure personal privacy, water supply hot and cold with a sewage disposal. The plumbing of a home in one piece can be limited to a toilet outside the dwelling provided that. This toilet is located in the same building and easily accessible.

6) A grid allowing sufficient lighting all Chambers and access and the operation household appliances essential to life daily. In dwellings located in the overseas departments, provisions for hot water under 4 and 5 above shall not apply.

Article 4

The housing has at least one main Chamber with representing a floor area not less than 9 square meters and a height equal to at least 2.20 meters habitable volume is at least equal to 20 cubic meters. The habitable surface area and volume are determined accordance with the second and third subparagraphs of Article R 111-2 of the Building Code and housing.

Article 5

Housing that is the subject of an order or unhealthy Risk cannot be regarded as decent housing.

Article 6

The improvement work provided for in Article 1 of the Law of 12 July 1967 referred to above are those whose sole purpose to the premises in compliance with all or part of provisions of Articles 1 to 4 of this Decree without reaching than those features which are defined.

Articles 1, 5 to 14 and 17 of the Decree of 9 November 1968

above are hereby repealed.
Article 7

The Keeper of the Seals, Minister of Justice, the Minister of Inside, the Minister for Infrastructure, Transport and housing, the Secretary of State for Overseas and Secretary State housing are responsible, each in respect of the, for the implementation of this Decree, which will be published Journal Official (JO) de la République française.
By the Prime Minister:
Lionel Jospin.
The Minister for Infrastructure, Transport and Housing, Jean
laude Gayssot.
The Keeper of the Seals, Minister of Justice,
Marylise Lebranchu.
The Minister of Interior,
Daniel Vaillant.
The Secretary of State for Overseas
Chistian Paul.
Secretary of State for Housing,
Marie-Noëlle Lienemann.

DOCUMENTARY REFERENCES

General works of synthesis or Building management, real estate edition Dalloz, 1995.
Tenant and owner - Act of 6 July 1989 - Edition Official Journal, may 2001.
The tenant and the home, edition, Juris-binder, 2002.
Code and leases condominiums, Dalloz, 1992, 1996, 2000 editions.
Code de l'urbanisme, Dalloz, 1990 edition.
Code de l'environnement, Dalloz, 1990 edition.
Journals (excerpts of articles: Real Estate & Court)
Gazette des communes (the)
Gazette du Palais (la)
Journal of bailiffs
Journal of Real Estate
Rental and condominium
Rent review
Journal of habitat
Official Bulletin of the Ministry of Infrastructure,
Transport and Housing
Official Bulletin of the Ministry of Justice
Bulletin of the civil judgments of the Supreme Court
Bulletin of the judgments of the Supreme Court in respect criminal
Official Bulletin of competition, consumption and prevent fraud
News (the) law, real property (known (until 1997)
News (the) legal, real estate law (known since 1998).

www.ingramcontent.com/pod-product-compliance
Lightning Source LLC
Chambersburg PA
CBHW071234170526
45165CB00003B/1092